PHILOSOPHICAL REFLECTIONS ON THE CHANGES IN EASTERN EUROPE

Philosophy and the Global Context

Series Editor: Michael Krausz, Bryn Mawr College

This new series addresses a range of emerging global concerns. It situates philosophical efforts in their global and cultural contexts, and it offers works from thinkers whose cultures are challenged by globalizing movements. Comparative and intercultural studies address such social and political issues as the environment, poverty, consumerism, civil society, tolerance, colonialism, global ethics, and community in cyberspace. They also address related methodological issues of translation and cross-cultural understanding.

Editorial Advisory Board
Ted Benton, University of Essex
David Crocker, University of Maryland
Fred Dallmayr, University of Notre Dame
Elliot Deutsch, University of Hawaii
Nancy Fraser, New School for Social Research
Jay Garfield, University of Tasmania
David Theo Goldberg, Arizona State University
Rom Harré, Georgetown University
Bernard Harrison, University of Utah
Ram Mall, University of Cologne
Joseph Margolis, Temple University
Jitendra Mohanty, Temple University
Ashis Nandy, Centre for the Study of Developing Societies, Delhi, India
Martha Nussbaum, University of Chicago
Amélie Oksenberg Rorty, Brandeis University
Mark Sagoff, University of Maryland
Ken-ichi Sasaki, University of Tokyo
Ofelia Schutte, University of Florida
Margarita Valdés, University of Mexico
Kwasi Wiredu, University of South Florida

Intellectual Property: Moral, Legal, and International Dilemmas (1997)
    by Adam D. Moore
Ethics of Consumption: The Good Life, Justice, and Global Stewardship (1998)
    edited by David A. Crocker and Toby Linden
Alternative Visions: Paths in the Global Village (1998)
    by Fred Dallmayr
Philosophical Reflections on the Changes in Eastern Europe (1998)
    by William L. McBride

PHILOSOPHICAL REFLECTIONS ON THE CHANGES IN EASTERN EUROPE

William L. McBride

ROWMAN & LITTLEFIELD PUBLISHERS, INC.
Lanham • Boulder • New York • Oxford

ROWMAN & LITTLEFIELD PUBLISHERS, INC.

Published in the United States of America
by Rowman & Littlefield Publishers, Inc.
4720 Boston Way, Lanham, Maryland 20706

12 Hid's Copse Road
Cumnor Hill, Oxford OX2 9JJ, England

Copyright © 1999 by Rowman & Littlefield Publishers, Inc.

All rights reserved. No part of this publication may be reproduced, stored in a retrieval system, or transmitted in any form or by any means, electronic, mechanical, photocopying, recording, or otherwise, without the prior permission of the publisher.

British Library Cataloguing in Publication Information Available

Library of Congress Cataloging-in-Publication Data

McBride, William L.
    Philosophical reflections on the changes in Eastern Europe / William L. McBride.
       p. cm.— (Philosophy and the global context)
    Includes bibliographical references and index.
    ISBN 0-8476-8797-X (hardcover : alk. paper)—ISBN 0-8476-8798-8 (pbk. : alk. paper)
    1. Europe, Eastern—Politics and government—1989- —Philosophy. 2. Post-communism—Europe, Eastern. 3. Social values—Europe, Eastern. 4. Social change—Europe, Eastern. I. Title.
JN96.A58M39   1999
947'.0009'049—dc21   98-35373
                                                                           CIP

Printed in the United States of America

∞ ™ The paper used in this publication meets the minimum requirements of American National Standard for Information Sciences—Permanence of Paper for Printed Library Materials, ANSI Z39.48–1984.

Contents

Acknowledgments		vii
Introduction		1
Chapter One	The Bygone Era	13
Chapter Two	Today	25
Chapter Three	Conversions and Continuities	47
Chapter Four	Theory and Practice: Philosophical Politicians and Philosophy as Political	65
Chapter Five	Values	81
Chapter Six	The Throne, the Altar, and the Cottage	105
Chapter Seven	Worldviews: From One Materialism to Another?	125
Index		135
About the Author		139

Acknowledgments

The idea of writing this book first came to me during a visit to Bulgaria and former Yugoslavia in summer 1990. I owe a debt of gratitude, then, to the organizers of the Summer School of Varna for having invited me to speak there, both in that year and in summer 1992. I am also indebted to the organizers, primarily faculty members of the University of Nikšić, of the special conference entitled "The Meaning of the Changes in Eastern Europe," which was held in Budva, Montenegro, in May 1991, just six weeks before Yugoslavia's bloody dissolution began. Thanks are likewise due to the Hegeler Foundation for supporting my participation in a conference called "Philosophy and Political Change in Eastern Europe" that was held in Budapest in March 1992; on the same trip, I enjoyed the hospitality of the philosophy faculty of the P. J. Safarik University in Prešov, Slovakia, as it celebrated the four hundredth anniversary of the birth of Jan Comenius. The Center for Humanitistic Studies of Purdue University's School of Liberal Arts awarded me a facilitating grant for fall 1993. My opportunity to speak and to exchange ideas at the Institute for Philosophical Research of the Bulgarian Academy of Sciences, Sofia, at Sofia University St. Kliment Ohridski; at the Democratic Center, Belgrade; and at the University of Miskolć, Hungary, in spring 1995, was abetted by a welcome travel grant from IREX (International Research and Exchanges Board). The Citizen Ambassador Program asked me to serve as group leader of a philosophy delegation to Russia and Hungary in fall 1995. Both the University of Zagreb and the Centre Eidos in Saint Petersburg, Russia, as well as Sofia University once again, hosted me in spring 1996. In spring 1997 I was an invitee of the American Cultural Center in Sofia, of the American University in Bulgaria, Blagoevgrad, which sponsored a conference called "Civil Society in South East Europe: Philosophical and Ethical Perspectives," which I keynoted, and of the University of Łódź, Poland, where I spent a delightful and instructive week. The second phase of the civil society conference was held at Rochester Institute of Technology in September 1997, and there I read a version of one chapter of the present book. I returned to Sofia University St. Kliment Ohridski for the fall 1997 term, where I held a Fulbright lectureship. During that period, I was also a guest of the Vernadsky Foundation for a conference, held in Dubna, on the prospects of Russia in the third millennium, as well as of the Institute of Philosophy of the Serbian Academy of Science, Belgrade, and once again of the American University in Bulgaria, Blagoevgrad; on both of the latter occasions, I also read versions of chapters of this book, the manuscript of which I completed while in Sofia. Finally, I returned to Sofia in April 1998 to give a public lecture summarizing some of its main points. To all of those who were responsible for these various invitations and the various kinds of support connected with them, my heartfelt thanks!

Many of these individuals are included in the following, no doubt incomplete, list of people to whom I am especially grateful for conversations and/or personal encouragement: Tatiana Batouleva (Sofia), Joseph Bien (Missouri), Elizabeth Bowman (New York), Joseph Catalano (New York), Alexander Chumakov (Moscow), Lilyana Deyanova (Sofia), Maria Dimitrova (Sofia), Nelly Dobreva (Sofia), Berta Dragićević (Dubrovnik), David Durst (Blagoevgrad), Istvan Fehér (Budapest), Gvozden Flego (Zagreb), Dane Gordon (Rochester), Vladimir Gradev (Sofia), Alexander Gungov (Sofia), Emilia Ivanova (Sofia), Alison Jaggar (Colorado), Andrzej Kaniowski (Łódź), Kasia Kaniowski (Łódź), Serge Konyaev (Moscow), Dragoljub Mićunović (Belgrade), Natalija Mićunović (Belgrade, former Purdue graduate student), Liubava Moreva (Saint Petersburg), J. Christoph Nyíri (Budapest), Lazar Popov (Sofia), Asija Prohić (Paris), Eleonora Prohić (Belgrade and Sarajevo), Gérard Raulet (Paris), Yvanka Raynova (Sofia and Vienna), Tom Rockmore (Pittsburgh), Svetozar Stojanović (Belgrade), and Robert Stone (New York).

I am also grateful to my Purdue colleagues for their support. I could name many, but will single out only a few for special mention: Philosophy Department Head Rodney Bertolet, Edith Clowes (foreign languages and literatures), Leonard Harris, Lewis Gordon (now at Brown), Martin Beck Matuštík, and Dean Margaret Moan Rowe, together with the philosophy department's peerless administrative assistant, Pamela Connelly, and a number of past and present graduate students, especially (in terms of discussions helpful for this book) Jeffrey Paris.

Finally, special recognition goes to the constant inspiration provided by my wife, Angela Barron McBride, and by our two children, Catherine McBride Chang and Kara Angela McBride.

Introduction

The collapse of an entire way of life that occurred in Eastern and Central Europe in, for the most part, late 1989 and 1990 must rank as one of the most astonishing events in the astonishing, often tragically astonishing, century that we shall soon be leaving.[1] Aristotle's often cited claim that all philosophy begins in wonder merits citation once more: If these events amaze us, as I think they should, then they are worthy of philosophical reflection. It was with this conviction that I began planning the present book some seven years ago.

My motivations for doing so were not just abstractly theoretical and detached. There were at least two other considerations. First, all of the regimes and hegemonic political parties that fell from power during these events claimed adherence to some version or other of Marxism. The *philosophy* of Marx—incomplete and riddled with problems of interpretation as we find it, and as thousands of books and hundreds of thousands of essays have discussed it—is one that I had studied in some detail and for which I had developed considerable sympathy in my early professional years.[2] That sympathy did not desert me. I never failed to distinguish between Marx's philosophy and official Marxist-Leninist ideology and practice, regarding the latter as in many respects a perversion of the former. But it cannot be said to have been so in *all* respects, of course, and then things become complicated. Some of these complications will be explored in the course of this book. But at any rate it became clear that, perverse as it might have seemed, the sudden banishment of the "perversions" of Marxism to the attic of history had resulted, very soon after the events of 1989–1990, in a considerable loss of interest in Marxism itself. And this development—an unhappy one, as I saw it—motivated me at least to try to understand its historical logic.

The other consideration was, from the start, personal. Although I share Aristotle's belief that "wonder" can be generated among a number of people (why else should what causes wonder in Aristotle interest me or anyone else?), I also subscribe to the more contemporary view that regards any worthwhile philosophy as being in some way rooted, and at best *consciously* rooted, in the philosopher's own lived experiences. For instance, Aristotle's interest in biological examples, and particularly in rather esoteric sea fauna, such as mollusks, must have had a lot to do with his early years in Stagira (on the Black Sea in modern northern Greece close to Turkey and Bulgaria) and with his father's profession, which was that of physician. It was not predetermined to work this way, of course; Aristotle might have avoided all mention of such matters, just as in his *Politics* he offers few hints that he had been a tutor in the Macedonian royal family that was in the process of overturning Greek political life through its conquests and its federating of the old city-states. But to know these background facts is both to know Aristotle better and to have, I believe, more, rather than less, basis for appreciating his philosophy. So I have no reluctance in acknowledging that my own past experiences had much to do with my beginning the present undertaking.

Eastern Europe did not preoccupy me greatly in my very early years. What was probably most decisive for me was an automobile trip that I undertook in summer 1960, after a year spent as a Fulbright scholar in France. I wanted to see Greece—the civilization of Aristotle was already very important to me—and to go there by car entailed traversing Yugoslavia. To do so then was quite an adventure: Most highways were unpaved and very rough, with twenty or twenty-five kilometers per hour considered a maximum safe speed over the majority of them. Moreover, the car that I had rented was defective, and the defect manifested itself on my first afternoon in the country, a Sunday, and forced me to spend the night in the Slovenian town of Vrhnika. (Vrhnika, the site of a Yugoslav National Army garrison, was featured in news stories at the outbreak of that country's civil war, but it was not itself a scene of great carnage.) The people were kind, especially a young man, apparently an official of minor rank, who found a private home to accommodate me. That night I fell to speaking with him, in my poor German, about the Yugoslav experiment in socialism.

There were still many idealists then, my first-night host among them. (By "idealists," I mean dedicated believers in communist ideals as they understood them and not alleged or actual subscribers to antimaterialist, or "idealist," versions of metaphysics and epistemology whom Communist Party ideologists were then hard at work denouncing throughout the Soviet Bloc.) Later on the same trip, I saw a group of teenagers walking out one morning to work on upgrading a road; at its head was a young woman carrying an enormous Yugoslav flag. Many who lived through those years may find that this scenario evokes nightmarish associations. Indeed, many in prisons did experience life as a nightmare during those same years. (In terms of numbers, and as a rough generalization not applicable everywhere, the early 1950s had probably been a worse period.) But I doubt that all (or most or possibly any) of the members of that teenage workforce viewed themselves as living a nightmare at the time; on the contrary, it was for them no doubt a worthwhile, patriotic summer adventure.

Over the years, my personal contacts with Eastern Europeans multiplied. As a graduate student back in the United States, I made the acquaintance of visiting members of the *Praxis* group of Yugoslav philosophers. Through these acquaintances I eventually came to know a number of their colleagues as well. Although their specific philosophical backgrounds and interests varied somewhat, they seemed to share, in large measure, a common outlook; later, as the country began to fall apart, they were to follow quite divergent political paths. In subsequent years, I traveled as a tourist through several East European countries, notably Czechoslovakia, Hungary, and Poland; I first visited the last country, for example, in the fascinating year of its "millennium" (1966), when state and church were openly fighting over the issue of which had more reason to claim the event as its own. (The baptism of the Polish king in 966 had obtained recognition for the Polish state as a legitimate regime, no longer just a "tribe.") In more recent years, I have made frequent trips of a professional nature.

I had originally intended to write nothing directly about these visits, but I have come to think that a few of them may be worth recounting briefly for their potential relevance to my subject matter. There follow, then, five vignettes in chronological sequence, three from the time just before the watershed events of late 1989 and two from subsequent years. In May 1988, I was invited to attend a conference in Poland on philosophical approaches to nature.[3] It took place on the grounds of an ancient monastery that had been converted into a country inn, hence in an informal atmosphere in which some unofficial dialogue was possible. One evening, when the topic of conversation turned to recent governmental suppressions of strikes sponsored by the Solidarity labor leadership, I hesitantly asked a graduate student conference organizer, whom I considered especially astute, whether he thought that there was a future for the Solidarity movement in his country. He said that he thought not, unfortunately, although perhaps in ten years a new movement sharing some of Solidarity's ideas might arise and have a chance of success. At that time Poland was still a self-styled "socialist" state and the Communist leaderships of Eastern Europe were all still in place, although a major resignation—by the Hungarian leader, Kadar—took place that very week.

Two months later I had the privilege of attending a small philosophy gathering in Budapest on the general topic of ideality and reality.[4] Economic reform, though small by comparison with what was to come, had already advanced further in Hungary than in the other Central and Eastern European countries, with the exception of the special case of Yugoslavia. But the philosophy department of the Eötvös Lorand University, like so many other Hungarian official institutions, was still formally dedicated to Marxism-Leninism. That the reality was indeed vastly at odds with the official ideal was illustrated in an anecdote, told by our host, Professor J. C. Nyíri, at the time in charge of the history of philosophy section, concerning a conversation that he had had with one of the higher education authorities the previous fall. The latter had asked our colleague what he thought about the future prospects of Marxist philosophy in Hungary. Nyíri had replied that they were excellent, in his opinion, because the status of Marxism could not sink any lower than it already had. Nyíri pointed out that his witticism had been slightly risky from a political standpoint at that time, although it had ceased to be so by the following summer as we were meeting.

In spring 1989 I attended the annual spring seminar, "Marxismus und Phänomenologie," at the Inter-University Centre in Dubrovnik. The climate of opinion was changing very rapidly. It was the last year, as far as I could ascertain from a later perusal of the next two years' schedules, in which Marxism was considered to be an acceptable component of seminar titles at that important center for international meetings, whereas in earlier years Marxism had been a staple topic there. Over the weekend between the sessions, I journeyed to Sarajevo to speak to a meeting of the Association Franco-Yougoslave on the subject of the reception of Jean-Paul Sartre's work in the United States.[5] I gave my talk in the building of the liberal arts faculty of the University of Sarajevo. During this period, inflation, although later it was largely controlled until the outbreak of the war, was running rampant. There was so much talk of dividing up the country that I told friends upon my return that Yugoslavia would soon cease to exist. I doubt that many, if any, of the scholars with whom I associated during that time would have predicted that within three years both the Inter-University Centre building and the liberal arts faculty building in Sarajevo would be in ruins or that most or all of those in my Sarajevo audience would have become, in one grim way or another, war victims.

Then came the "world-historical" events of summer and fall 1989. Following them from across the Atlantic, I felt pleased about the end of the most salient forms of oppression of almost all the East European peoples and especially the East Germans; the quixotic, almost fairy-tale–like rise to ascendancy of Václav Havel; and in general the development of attitudes of tolerance, of democracy in the most fundamental sense of mutual human respect, and of greater interest in and accessibility to Western Europe and the rest of the world—all of which were immediately perceivable. But my pleasure was offset by feelings of deep foreboding and pessimism, as reports came back of widespread, generally unreflective enthusiasm for "the market," for Western-style consumerism, and in general for the Reagan-Thatcher era equating individual selfishness (technically understood, of course, as the driving force of "the market") with the will of God, or at least the will of History,[6] in the newly liberated lands. The enormous deviation of socialism[7] that had been the Soviet Bloc East European "experiment" was at the time still the prevailing, though rapidly decaying, system in the USSR itself. It had left most of its victims with a revulsion for the very idea of socialism. And a great many of them had turned, in psychologically understandable but shockingly naive trust, to an extreme, idealized version (more extreme than that actually practiced in the United States or anywhere else) of capitalism as their salvation.

Despite my forebodings, it now seems clear to me that I was naive at the time. I did not, for example, anticipate the colonization—the term is common coin in the country itself—of millions of East Germans by privileged "Wessis," including the massive, self-serving replacement of East German philosophers and other intellectuals in academic positions by West Germans on the ground that the former must by definition be ideologically unacceptable. Neither did I anticipate the repudiation of Havel's vision by a majority of his fellow citizens and the ensuing division of the former Czechoslovakia itself, nor the rise to prominence in numerous states, east and west, of intolerance toward minorities and foreigners in general. Where "democracy" is still invoked with applause and enthusiasm, it all too often serves now as a cover for new oppressions,[8] as it did in the days of the "German Democratic Republic" and all the other "Democratic" Communist regimes of former times. In short, much of the 1989 optimism, limited as it was, turns out to have been exaggerated.

In summer 1990 I attended the School of Varna on the Black Sea in Bulgaria. My week there left me with a pastiche of impressions of a country trying to deal peacefully with the most fundamental changes in all sorts of assumptions about political and social life, from the abstract and general to the everyday. Elections were being held, in the usual two-round sequence that is common in Western Europe. Street disturbances had broken out in Sofia after the results of the first round had showed considerable support remaining for the Socialist Party, the reformed former Communist Party. I was struck by the resilience of individuals and by their capacity to carry on under such radically changed circumstances—even to carry on the strange activity of philosophy! It was this occasion, more than any other, that led to the present book. The idea came to me of reconsidering the meaning of fundamental social change, the topic of my first book,[9] now that I was observing an actual instance of it close-up, and to rethink what the possibility and reality of such change might imply concerning some larger philosophical questions. At Varna, I also had my first extended discussions with a Bulgarian philosopher, Yvanka Raynova, whose detailed knowledge of intellectual life in Bulgaria impressed me greatly and led to my collaborating with her several years later in an article that she wrote on philosophical life in Bulgaria. It was first published in a volume entitled *Philosophy and Political Change in Eastern Europe*.[10]

My final set of vignettes returns me to Yugoslavia, or rather "former Yugoslavia." I was once again at the Inter-University Centre in Dubrovnik in April 1991 to attend the phenomenology seminar, which had been resumed after a year's hiatus but without, as I have noted, any mention of "Marxismus" in its title. Most of the Yugoslav newspapers had intensified their ethnic biases and slurs, and memories of old ethnic massacres from the end of the Second World War and earlier were being revived. The political breakup of the country now seemed quite imminent, and some feared the worst. But many others, including very knowledgeable philosopher-politicians and political analysts of my acquaintance, still believed in the reasonable possibility of some compromise; I vividly remember several discussions to this effect. This remained the state of affairs near the end of the following month, when I attended a conference in Budva, Montenegro, on (quite ironically, in retrospect) the significance of the changes throughout Eastern Europe.[11] True, the day on which I traveled from Belgrade to Montenegro had been, by all accounts, a fateful day: a majority of the members of the so-called Yugoslavian "presidency" had voted against the normally routine rotation of the chair of that group to the Croatian representative, Mešić, who had been in line to hold it for the following year. But even then, on the eve of the war as it turned out (major hostilities began a little more than a month later), there were still many who anticipated some compromise or at least did not really anticipate the full-scale conflagration that was to ensue.[12]

The events that occasioned my original project of undertaking this book have had important effects on friends of mine, which would have affected me profoundly even in the absence of all philosophical considerations. Aristotle, poised to attack Plato's doctrines with a heavy intellectual bludgeon, wrote that truth is more important than friendship, though he may have had some qualms about treating his old master in this way. I now think that this is much too glib. Although one may try to argue one's friends into accepting what one believes to be true, it would be boring and unfortunate if they always gave in. Moreover, I confess to thinking that the engaged and cordial interaction that is friendship is more important to a human being than the possession of absolute truth, even if the latter were possible. So I began this book thinking that I would try to see in part through the eyes of, and on behalf of, *friends* who have been deeply involved in its theme, though I expected full agreement from none of them.

What do I hope then to accomplish with the "reflections" herein? A reconsideration of some of the claims made in the opening paragraph of this introduction will help provide an answer. The changes of 1989–1990 were, taken as a whole, exceedingly fundamental. Few would question this, though experts would point out, quite correctly, that the revolution was less dramatic in some places than in others, for various reasons. Perhaps Czechoslovakia, or at least the "Czech Republic" portion of that now divided state, should be seen as the site of the most complete and rapid change of all, though even here—because the notion of an "absolute change" in the real world of the political is nonsensical—numerous elements of the old order remained through the transition. In Hungary, for example, the changes were less dramatic because some of them had already been initiated under the socialist government. In Bulgaria, to take another example, the former Communist, renamed Socialist, Party actually won the parliamentary elections of spring 1990 that eventuated from the ouster of former dictator Zhivkov; it later lost control of parliament, then regained it several years later, then lost it again in a rather humiliating way after the massive peaceful demonstrations of February 1997. And so on. Each case is different, and in no case, obviously, is the story of the transition as yet "complete." (It *never* is, of course.) But to focus exclusively on the real elements of continuity across the changes is to miss the most salient fact, which is the changes! Just so, it would be silly to deny the enormous historical impact of Russia's October Revolution of 1917 just because so many of its goals have now been repudiated.

Changes of such magnitude must be explainable. That is the presupposition here, and so explanation of a certain type must be an important goal. There are very different sorts of explanations, of course, and there is a value in being as tolerant as possible of all of them. I no longer feel the scorn that I felt in my college years when told that a very intelligent upperclassman, when challenged by an outside board that was examining him in connection with an important prize to name the principal cause or causes of World War I, answered "original sin." That may have been an answer worth exploring, but it was a very complex one, depending on an entire theoretical framework concerning the human condition. At any rate, my focus here will be on *explananda*—phenomena appearing to require an explanation—that seem most interesting to me as a philosopher and on those explanations of them that seem most plausible, without thereby excluding others. (For example, a journalistic account of the events in question—what the Czech police did, how large elements of the population responded, and so on—is no doubt quite valuable. But I regard the task of explaining what happened at such an episodic level to be for the most part the province of others.) I readily admit the prevalence and even the dominance of the seemingly nonrational in human affairs—for example, the tragic earthquake that without forewarning destroys thousands of human hopes and projects in a few seconds. I believe that the nonrational can also be woven into an account that can be understood and communicated, at least as long as it has to do with human action. Even insane conduct has its intelligible side.

Although the changes that occurred were astonishing, they were also predictable; that is, given data known to all in early 1989, including known facts about possible ways in which crowds, police, government officials, and so on may sometimes act, they could have been predicted. As far as I know, however, they generally were not. At the time, we were all astonished. Only later did some writers and thinkers begin to look back, *post festum*, and point out signs and symptoms that had been there to see. There is nothing dishonest or otherwise wrong about this, and many of my reflections in this book rely in part on such hindsight. But the proposition that traditional Communist Party dominance in Eastern Europe would end within a matter of just a few months was not one that anyone, to the best of my knowledge, was seriously advancing even shortly before the end came.

The changes have affected an entire way of life, not just political regimes. They have reached down deep into people's everyday activities, occasioning bewildered questions like one I overheard asked by an ordinary citizen complaining about procedures at an ordinary post office in the former East Berlin during a period when the assimilation of the two Germanies was still far from complete: "Ist das Sozialismus oder ist das Kapitalismus?" Some things did not change. For example, private apartments (unless returned to former owners or their heirs, as has been the case in some parts of the former Eastern Bloc) retain the same furnishings, most households maintain the same routines as before, and other important banalities. But so many expectations in regard to the sphere of public or community activities have been drastically altered or simply reversed.

In my view it is philosophically indefensible, however, to take the facile and popular route of simply identifying the old, vanished way of life as "bad" and the new, supposedly democratic one as "good." The world does not exist in black and white alone. The old regimes were "totalitarian," granted, if by that one means thoroughgoing in their effects on people's lives and in their aspirations to control major parts of them. Although the new regimes generally allow a greater scope for individual choice in various areas, they are no less thoroughgoing in many of their effects for all that; in adopting free market economic mechanisms, for example, they have not left it up to individuals to decide whether they want to play by the new economic rules or the old ones or some third option. Likewise, the old regimes resulted in the often hypocritical (because contrary to stated socialist ideals) privileging of the *nomenklatura*, the Communist Party elite, of course; but does anyone pretend that the new regimes have not already dramatically privileged certain groups, particularly certain groups of "entrepreneurs," over others along lines that have nothing to do with justice or fairness, however that is construed? These are among the issues that are considered in the course of this book. My point is not to lament the demise of the old regimes as such, but merely to indicate a few of the most obvious reasons underlying the by now familiar reaction that things have not turned out to be nearly as positive and unproblematic as they may have appeared to cheerleaders of the changes during their earliest phase. My ultimate hope is that the philosophical analyses here will contribute something toward an understanding of this development.

I proceed along the following lines. In chapter 1, I attempt to reconstruct something of the prechange climate of thought and activity in the countries of Eastern Europe. There existed in all of them, with different degrees of emphasis in different countries and at different times, an official ideology that claimed Marx as its progenitor. In chapter 2, I assemble some observations (anything more systematic at this point would be simply foolhardy and misleading) about the recent and current climates, always taking account of the enormous (and in many respects increasing) variabilities from one country to the next and, within the same country, from one month to the next. The fact of extreme variability leads me, in chapter 3, to explore my first central philosophical issue—what I call, for brevity, "conversions." How is it possible, and what does it mean, for serious thinkers to make the transition, often very rapidly, from one set of deeply held and strongly defended philosophical beliefs to another set that appears diametrically opposite to the first? Such transitions *seem* commonplace, though of course not universal, in the countries in question. Moreover, some of those who have made such transitions have advanced from theory to political practice, a move that Marxism was once famous for advocating. An astonishingly large segment of important political figures in post-Communist Eastern Europe has consisted of philosophers and of intellectuals with philosophically related interests. In chapter 4, then, I explore, in light of the Eastern European experience, this old phenomenon of philosophers in politics (Plato once involved himself deeply in the politics of distant Syracuse, for example)—its rationale and its chances of success. Whatever these chances may be, it is clear that the *rationale* for political involvement must always be based on certain *values*, and it is the topic of values and their major and rapid transvaluation in the Eastern Europe of the past decade—in other words, what values are, and what may remain of them—that is my central concern in chapter 5. This concern carries over into chapter 6, in which I deal with three sets of phenomena and practices productive of values that clearly either remain viable or have become newly viable for substantial numbers of people in Eastern Europe today. At the same time, they are often regarded, with good reason, as creative of severe *dis*values and harm: nationalism, religion, and human relationships, especially those associated with the family (as in the expression "family values") and with the treatment of women. Finally, in my concluding chapter, I take a brief look at "ultimate things," notions of what is ultimately real and/or important. Marxist-Leninist ideology had a clear (at least superficially clear) vision of what that was—matter, construed dialectically and in terms of a certain historical sequence ("diamat"/"histomat"). Now, along with the widely noted revivals of nationalism and religion, which differ greatly, to be sure, depending on the milieu and are by no means general, Eastern Europe is also experiencing a very widespread revival of "materialism" of another sort—consumerist materialism that was once associated primarily with the West. I believe that this reference to the two kinds of materialism is more than just a play on words and reflects important beliefs, on both sides of the distinction, about what human existence across historical time ultimately means and is. I conclude with a few reflections about this.

This is not a book of history, and I do not pretend to be comprehensive concerning the events that have occasioned these reflections, nor even to be basing my reflections on a sort of "average" or "median" reading of what has happened, on the whole, in the countries in question. At the same time, I try to maintain balance and avoid one-sidedness in my reporting of these events, which serve as the essential background to my reflections. The core of what I shall have to say resides in those reflections themselves—the reflections of a philosopher (construe the word however you wish!) interested above all in the kinds of questions in which philosophers have always been interested.

Introduction 11

Notes

1. The terminology used here is of considerable importance for many residents of the region. In former Yugoslavia, in particular, but elsewhere in Europe as well, reference is often made to a supposed "fault line" dividing *Eastern* Europe from *Central* Europe, a "line" that derives much of its alleged reality from the ancient religious division between Orthodox and Roman Catholic Christianity. On the other hand, the application of the term "Eastern Europe" to *all* the countries of the Warsaw Pact, also called the "Eastern Bloc," including East Germany, was a commonplace during the entire post-World War II era (when Yugoslavia, as a nonsignatory to the Warsaw Pact, was considered, and rightly so, to be anomalous). Now there even exists a terminological trend in the direction of developing new (or newly revived), more subtle geographical designations, often involving somewhat new regional groupings. The expression "South East Europe" is a salient example of this. In what follows I sometimes follow the convention "Eastern and Central Europe," without thereby implying any particular belief about the reality or unreality of the alleged "fault line," apart from undisputed historical facts. Just as often I simply use the shorthand expression in this book's title, "Eastern Europe," hoping that it will be understood that I intend no offense to anyone except those who employ the "fault line" idea in a racist way, as a term of contempt for certain ethnicities.

2. William L. McBride, *The Philosophy of Marx* (London: Hutchinson; and New York: St. Martin's, 1977).

3. William L. McBride, "Sartre and the Philosophy of Ecology," *Mensch—Natur—Kosmos, Acta Universitatis Lodziensis,* Folia Philosophica 8 (1991): 69–80.

4. A portion of the proceedings of this conference, along with some other material, appears in J. C. Nyíri, ed., *Perspectives on Ideas and Reality* (Budapest: Filozófiai Posztgraduális és Információs Központ, 1990).

5. This paper, in French, remains unpublished. A tape of an interview that Eleonora Prohić conducted with me, with a voice-over in Serbo-Croatian, interspersed with her 1969 interview with Sartre in Dubrovnik, was distributed and shown throughout Yugoslavia in mid-April 1989. At that time cooperative exchanges of such tapes among the television services of the various republics were still the rule. Simultaneously, a story dealing with the topic of the paper that I presented at Dubrovnik, an ironic reprise of certain events and discussions of revolution in the United States in 1968 in light of the bicentenary of the French Revolution, appeared in the Zagreb journal *Danas* ("Konzervativni Autsajderi," 18 April 1989, written by Jasmina Kuzmanović). I told friends that, for a one-week period (Warhol's fifteen minutes of fame slightly extended), I was probably the best-known American philosopher in Yugoslavia, and that in a few years people to whom I mentioned this would be asking what Yugoslavia had been. One could still maintain a little humor about the situation at that time.

6. I am thinking here of Francis Fukuyama's book *The End of History and the Last Man* (New York: Free Press, 1992), which enjoyed considerable, though brief, popularity. See my article "The Phenomenological Tradition and

the End of History" in *Phenomenology and Skepticism: Essays in Honor of James M. Edie,* ed. Brice M. Wachterhauser (Evanston: Northwestern University Press, 1996), 180–90.

7. This ("deviation") is the central theme of the main completed portion of the posthumously published second volume of Jean-Paul Sartre's *Critique of Dialectical Reason.*

8. Recall, for instance, that it was the Serbian Democratic Party of Bosnia (not to be confused with the more genuinely democratic Democratic Party of Serbia itself) that dominated the self-styled government and militia that were guilty of so many atrocities in Bosnia.

9. William L. McBride, *Fundamental Change in Law and Society: Hart and Sartre on Revolution* (The Hague: Mouton, 1970).

10. William McBride and Ivanka Raynova, "Visions from the Ashes: Philosophical Life in Bulgaria from 1945 to 1992," in *Philosophy and Political Change in Eastern Europe,* ed. Barry Smith (LaSalle, Ill.: Monist Library of Philosophy, 1993), 103–33. At one point, consideration was given to the possibility of extending this collaboration to the present project by publishing our respective reflections on the changes in Eastern Europe in a single book, but this idea was later abandoned for logistical reasons.

11. William L. McBride, "Capitalism and Socialism and the New World Order: An American Perspective," *Luča* [journal of the University of Nikšić] 9, no. 1 (1992): 83-89. The issue is devoted to the proceedings of that conference.

12. A strong case against the belief that the conflict in Yugoslavia was inevitable is made in an article written by Belgrade philosopher Zagorka Golubović, "The Condition Leading to the Breakdown of the Yugoslav State: What Has Generated the Civil War in Yugoslavia?" *Praxis International* 12, no. 2 (1992): 129–44.

Chapter One

The Bygone Era

In the introduction I have referred to an account, which I authored jointly with Yvanka Raynova of the Institute of Philosophical Sciences of the Bulgarian Academy of Sciences, of philosophical life in Bulgaria during the nearly half century between the end of World War II and the peaceful end of the "totalitarian" regime in November 1989. It is in a sense a case study, and I continue to insist that each actual national "case" is different and unique. Universities of the German Democratic Republic, for instance, were reputedly more doctrinaire in enforcing Marxist-Leninist "orthodoxy" than those of almost any other "fraternal" country of the so-called Eastern Bloc, despite the long tradition of famous philosophers, such as Leibniz, who had once lived in the cities of that now extinct nation. Poland had had its distinctive schools of logic (e.g., Lukasziewicz's) and phenomenology (e.g., Ingarden's) before the war; the Hungarian philosophical situation cannot be understood apart from both the influence of Lukács and his followers and the calamity of the overt Soviet military invasion in 1956; philosophy in Czechoslovakia, which had begun to flourish, suffered especially severe devastation as a result of the Soviet intervention of 1968; and so on. Nevertheless, there was enough commonality of atmosphere in all of these countries during the long postwar Communist era to make some valid generalizations possible across the various individual narratives. This is what we attempted to do at several points in our recounting (a very unequal labor, Raynova's having been far more extensive than mine) of the Bulgarian story.

Story? Narratives? This very language, made popular by recent ("postmodern" and other) developments in Western philosophy, is already redolent of a radically different approach to thinking about the world from the one sanctioned by the official orthodoxy of the bygone era. Marxism, taking a lead from Hegel's thought in this regard as in so many others, treated *history* as an appropriate domain for theoretical generalization. Historical narrative, then, could be seen as an important ingredient in philosophy rather than, as a long tradition going back at least as far as Aristotle would have had it, either irrelevant or opposed to it.[1] Not satisfied with merely sanctioning the application of critical philosophical analysis to historical developments, however, orthodox Marxism-Leninism claimed to have discovered a set of true theoretical generalizations about history, by contrast with which all other equally sweeping generalizations, such as Hegel's view of history as the unfolding of divine justice through Spirit's self-discovery of the possibilities of its own freedom, were at best highly distortive and hence false. This truth was supposedly epitomized in certain formulas of the classics of Marx and Engels, beginning with the *Communist Manifesto*'s opening assertion that the history of all hitherto existing societies (or at least of all postprimitive societies, as Engels qualified it in a later footnote based on his newfound belief in the existence of some primitive cultures with communist social arrangements) has been the history of class struggle.[2] This is in fact a very interesting perspective on human history, no doubt important and to some significant extent veridical. But to regard it as merely one especially valuable perspective—one useful narrative account of history among others—was not enough for the guardians of Marxist-Leninist orthodoxy. They took it, this story of the class struggle, along with appropriate elaborations and further explanations, to be the absolute and supreme truth about world history. Other narratives about history either had to be dismissed as false or incorporated into subordinate positions within this one.

Once having assured themselves of the correctness of this position, the ideological proponents of Marxism-Leninism generally took one further step that is not in fact a logically necessary consequence of that conviction but seemed so to many of them: Views in conflict with the allegedly absolute truth about history should be suppressed as much as feasible, especially among intellectual leaders such as philosophers. The chief practical problem, besides that of deciding to just what extent suppression could conveniently be enforced, was then to identify the ideological chain of command, the chief arbiter of correct interpretation and his (it was never, in point of fact, her) designated lieutenants. V. I. Lenin was the first to resolve this problem by appointing himself (with the aid, of course, of allies and complicated political maneuvering) the arbiter and by furnishing flawed but plausible justifications, within the framework of the theory. He did so by means of such doctrines as "democratic centralism" (all to adhere unswervingly to decisions once reached after debate within the leadership) and, most fundamentally, by anointing the Communist Party (Bolsheviks) as the vanguard of the proletarian class in history's most decisive, final class struggle. (An intellectually more sophisticated, though logically perhaps even more flawed, version of this justificatory move was that devised in the 1920s by Georg Lukács when he depicted the party as the *imputed* bearer of the class consciousness of the proletariat.)[3] Lenin's example was of course followed, and his justificatory arguments even further simplified and tightened, by Stalin and, to varying degrees, his successors as well as by the postwar national Communist Party leaders in Eastern Europe. And so it came about that the lives particularly of intellectuals in this part of the world were strongly affected, and in many instances simply *dominated*, by fear of the consequences of deviating from whatever was proclaimed at any given time as constituting "the party line."

This outcome of Communist Party hegemony was by no means inevitable. Lenin's and Lukács' contemporary, Karl Korsch, in his *Marxism and Philosophy*,[4] had proposed treating Marxist theory as heuristic. For example, the category of social class could be conceived of as a guiding thread for achieving a deeper understanding of history, as well as for social practice, without being treated as the final solution to "the riddle of history."[5] But Korsch was thoroughly repudiated by the international Communist leadership, which proceeded to develop, consistently with the absolutist doctrine that I have described, a *catechetical* approach to Marxist-Leninist theory. (It is of interest to note that the *Communist Manifesto* itself had originally been planned by Engels to follow a catechetical style [Q: What is communism? A: Communism is . . .] instead of the rhetorical style of the published version.)[6] Postwar Eastern Europe was the arena for thousands and thousands of courses generally entitled "dialectical materialism," or "diamat" for short, in which the "truths" of this comprehensive worldview were systematically articulated in this rote, essentially unreflective way. There were also, of course, a number of "authoritative" textbooks published to be used in these courses and elsewhere. A relatively late but fairly typical example from the Soviet Union itself is Yuri A. Kharin's *Fundamentals of Dialectics*,[7] which found its way into English translation. Something of its flavor can be sensed in the following lines of a review of it that I was commissioned to write for the journal *Teaching Philosophy*:

> So that there can be no doubt as to where the author stands, Chapter I begins with the following sentence: "As the philosophy of the working class, Marxist-Leninist philosophy is the extreme form of materialism, a logical result of the preceding development of philosophical thought through the ages, and of the whole spiritual culture of mankind."[8]

Meanwhile, in Western countries, major efforts were undertaken to comprehend and report on the new political religion to the East. Some such efforts were made, particularly during the 1930s, by persons sympathetic to the Communist movement, such as (in those days) Sydney Hook.[9] During the postwar period of the "Cold War," and particularly during the briefer McCarthy era of political heresy hearings and trials in the United States, considerable writing and teaching about Marxism-Leninism and about Communism (the conceptual distinction between them must be retained in order to avoid confusion, although it was usually neglected by these writers and teachers) was done under the slogan—sometimes implicit, sometimes explicit—Know your enemy! Courses on "communism, fascism, and democracy" were the rage for a time in American colleges and universities. There were also some more serious, scholarly attempts to reconstruct and interpret Marxist-Leninist doctrine (as well as its history) with a certain degree of "objectivity," however elusive as a concept and questionable as an ideal this notion may be. Writers based in Western Europe, including several members of the Catholic clergy (e.g., Wetter, Calvez, Bochenski),[10] were prominent among such interpreters. In France in particular, the existence of a very large Communist Party with, somewhat paradoxically, both a tradition of intellectual engagement and an internally enforced spirit of more militant and doctrinaire adherence to Marxist-Leninist orthodoxy than in comparable countries such as Italy, provided a literature readily accessible to Western scholars that facilitated their articulation of the "enemy" doctrine.

But the spirit of Korsch and of the numerous and diverse other heretics who had dissented from the established orthodoxy (itself somewhat shifting and unstable, as illustrated by Stalin's overnight repudiation of the previously accepted linguistic theory of N. Y. Marr),[11] while still believing that there were ideas of great philosophical value and validity contained in the writings of Marx himself, never died. The expression "Western Marxism" has been devised as a cover term for a number of such writers, but it is not very precise (e.g., just how "Western" was the Hungarian Lukács?)[12] or, perhaps, very helpful. In any event, the growth and development of alternative Marxisms was greatly abetted by the dissemination of Marx's so-called early writings, particularly of the year 1844, which had for years lain undiscovered in archives. They were first published in small German and Russian editions that were then suppressed by Hitler and Stalin, respectively, during the 1930s, and only slowly came to be widely known and translated during the years following World War II. As contrasted with *Capital* and with the well-known popularizations of Marxist theory written by Marx's collaborator, Engels, these early works emphasize the effects of allegedly exploitative capitalist practices on the life worlds of human actors, envision the possibilities of a radically different, utopian society of the future, and take a less deterministic view of human behavior. Their less deterministic perspective is encapsulated in the Greco-German word *praxis* or "practice," suggesting active agency as opposed to passive receptivity, upon which Marx had focused in his brief, posthumously published *Theses on Feuerbach* of 1845.[13] This term in turn was taken as a journal title by a group of Yugoslav philosophers during the 1960s and came to be the label by which they were identified as a group.

Like the Yugoslav regime in the realm of politics, the *Praxis* group played a very special role in the bygone era that I am recalling, though it often did so in opposition to the central Yugoslav government itself, which eventually terminated publication of the original journal. It must be remembered that the Yugoslav leader Marshal Tito had broken with Stalin in the late 1940s and decided to go his own way. Efforts were made to develop a distinctive form of economic organization for the country, to be known as socialist self-management, in sharp contrast to the centralized command economic system of the USSR and other countries of the Bloc. In addition to, and no doubt in part as a result of, this economic decentralization and the political decentralization associated with Yugoslavia's federative system of partially autonomous republics, a somewhat greater diversity of thought was made possible there. Probably the best-known senior philosophers in the original *Praxis* group were Mihailo Marković, of Belgrade, and Gajo Petrović, of Zagreb. They and their collaborators brought diverse Western philosophical movements together with Marxian-influenced perspectives, so that their journal was from the outset very different in tone from any other Eastern Bloc philosophical literature.[14] *Praxis* writers generally supported the *ideal* of self-management, from which the reality of Yugoslav economic practice tended over the years to become increasingly distant (though it is doubtful that the two were ever very close). They opposed Serbian, Croatian, and other regional nationalisms, which they saw as serious obstacles to the larger national future. On this point, at least, more recent events have shown that they were indisputably correct.

The national fates of East European countries, as they have evolved toward the end of the second millennium, bear little or no resemblance to the expectations of any philosophers (or other writers, for that matter) with whose works of the 1950s or 1960s I am familiar. The pessimists expected the most repressive, mind-destroying aspects of Soviet "totalitarianism" as it had evolved under Stalin's long reign to perdure in the countries in question and gradually to spread to other parts of the world, with resistance in the latter leading eventually to an unprecedented nuclear conflagration, perhaps terminal for the human race. (The quotation marks that I have placed around "totalitarianism" here indicate the problematic nature, to my way of thinking, of this neologism, which came to be wielded as a slogan that was and still is thought to obviate all need to reflect seriously on some very complex, albeit very tragic, sociopolitical realities. In some respects party and government control was indeed total, or virtually so, whereas in other respects it was not, as subsequent events demonstrated. And the fact that "totalitarian regime" has by now become a commonplace way, in Eastern European countries, of designating the *anciens régimes* of what I am here calling "the bygone era" does not *eo ipso* justify this usage either, at least not in serious works of analysis. There will be further discussion of this later.)[15] The optimists, of whom some members of the *Praxis* group, at least at certain stages of its early history, and their sympathizers in countries other than Yugoslavia[16] were salient examples, foresaw the possibility of an evolution of the self-styled "socialist" countries, and at the limit even of the Soviet Union itself, in the direction of greater freedom of thought and practice. Few, if any, predicted the unseemly and rather pathetic collapse and dissolution that we have witnessed.

The most significant marker events in Eastern Europe during the decades of the 1950s and 1960s were, almost certainly, Stalin's death in 1953; the Khrushchev "thaw" and subsequent Soviet suppression of one country, Hungary, where this thaw was deemed to have been carried too far in 1955–1956; and the crushing of the reform-minded Dubček regime in Czechoslovakia that had appeared as an especially brilliant beacon of hope during the year of attempted revolts generally led by young people in various parts of the world, 1968. Prior to 1956, it is fairly safe to generalize, a condition of extremely heavy intellectual repression, such as that described in some detail in the article on Bulgaria that I have cited, generally obtained in all the countries under consideration, with Yugoslavia constituting a *relative* exception. Khrushchev's "revelations" about Stalin's excesses permitted, to various degrees and through various mechanisms in different countries, a rapid movement toward freer intellectual exploration, though most of it remained comparatively cautious and putatively anchored within a Marxian intellectual framework. The Soviet intervention in Budapest, where members of the working class had played a prominent role in a short-lived revolt that had brought a moderate but independent socialist regime to power, slowed this development but did not entirely stifle it. For example, in Poland, which in fact came close to suffering the same fate as Hungary in that year (Soviet ships stood ready to blockade Polish ports if Khrushchev were to order it, etc.), students and intellectuals began talking more about "democracy" again, and the government's repeated reversions to more reactionary policies over more than three subsequent decades never entirely erased the effects of this.

There were—again, to varying degrees in different countries—some contacts with Western thought and even with Western thinkers. On this point, once more, the Bulgarian case is suggestive. The party leaderships, given the logic of their self-imposed positions, denominated all Western philosophy "anti-Marxist," "bourgeois," "reactionary," and even (though there was at least some disagreement on this) "imperialist." At best, the study of non-Marxist thought subsequent to Marx was justified on a "know your enemy" basis that was the mirror image of the attitudes of some Western advocates of Cold War courses on Communism, but it was increasingly pursued by some of the best philosophical minds. (There existed additional historical arguments in favor of teaching the philosophies of some obvious antecedents to Marx, such as Aristotle and Hegel, but even in these cases it was generally deemed most important to emphasize their shortcomings.) However, these concessions created considerable ambivalence, since a philosophical "enemy" is unknowable in the absence of considerable communication with it, *at least* in the form of printed texts. Furthermore, it was a matter of pride to most party leaderships that their philosophers could participate *pari passu* with Western philosophers in major international congresses—where, the leadership hoped, the best Marxist-Leninists could vindicate the superiority of their position. An excellent example of this climate of ambivalence concerning Western thought is the meeting of the quinquennial World Congress of Philosophy in Varna, Bulgaria, in 1973, the only such meeting in a country of the Soviet Bloc. Members of the less "reliable" younger generation of Bulgarian philosophers were virtually excluded from the main activities there. Once again, it is important to recognize that the "totalitarianism" of the system, real and meaningful as it is in one sense, was in another sense not truly absolute—in the area of ideas any more than in the area of commodity and currency exchange.

For philosophers and some other intellectuals, Yugoslavia served as an important site for such ideological intermingling. During the middle 1960s, the summer school of Korčula, an island off the Adriatic coast, served as a meeting-place for Europeans with some interest in the Marxian tradition from both Western and Eastern countries. The invasion of Czechoslovakia in 1968 effectively put an end to most East European participation in the school, which itself was suppressed by Yugoslav authorities in 1974. However, the Inter-University Centre of Dubrovnik, supported by contributions from a number of non-Yugoslav (mostly Western European and U.S.) universities, began serving a somewhat similar function at about this time and continued to do so until the onset of the political changes throughout Eastern Europe, followed soon thereafter by the center's physical destruction in the war in late 1991. (The outer walls survived, and the interior of it has since been rebuilt.)[17] Although the number of participants, especially from other East European countries, in these gatherings and other academic meetings elsewhere in Yugoslavia was no doubt small by most reckonings, their contribution to the general process of thought adulteration in the East should not, in my opinion, be underestimated. Such events, taking place in a country whose regime considered itself communist but whose most prominent intellectuals debated and questioned "orthodox" Marxism-Leninism instead of simply accepting its truth, were more accessible than conferences in the West to a certain number of East European academics during at least certain periods. The more rigidly "orthodox" Marxist-Leninists found it all rather worrisome. Those who yearned for a different climate of thought, however, were encouraged. For example, although I make the claim with no written documentation but only verbal confirmation from some Bulgarian and American philosophers with long memories, the establishment of the rival school of Varna, not to be confused with the World Congress that took place there, was in part motivated by concern over the apparent success of the Korčula school. In short, a number of disparate factors—its location, its predominantly Slavic languages, its soft currency and easier visa requirements, and so on—facilitated Yugoslavia's playing something of a Trojan horse role (although the metaphor is of course inexact) within the Eastern Europe of the bygone era that we are recalling.

But there was another, more nebulous but undoubtedly far more central, phenomenon at work everywhere. Over the years, the societies of the Soviet Bloc countries came to be characterized by an overwhelming, all-pervasive cynicism. If philosophy is, as Hegel said with some truth, its own time apprehended in thoughts,[18] then the professional philosophers and other intellectuals of these societies came to incarnate this cynicism most fully and often very self-consciously. Even the most ordinary citizens were well aware of the enormous special privileges enjoyed, regardless of merit, by many government and party officials, simply by virtue of belonging to the Party hierarchy, the *nomenklatura*, that Milovan Djilas had so early and accurately labeled the "New Class."[19] For those who had ever aspired to understand the world more deeply and to find at least tentative and partial explanations, the situation was in many respects worse than it was for ordinary citizens from a psychological standpoint: The practical need to subordinate this aspiration to the changing requirements of the "party line" if one wished to retain any role whatever in intellectual life had the effect, as one of Kafka's characters aptly expresses it, of turning lying into a universal principle.[20] At the same time, the party line was officially defended as an extension or implementation of the "true" philosophy that is Marxism-Leninism, or even Marxism *tout court*—a ploy made easier, in a supreme irony, by the Marxian tradition's insistence on the very close interconnection of theory and practice. By the end of the forty-plus-year period in question, virtually no one—ordinary individual, intellectual, or party official—sincerely believed in the validity of this manipulative, opportunistic way of thinking. Consequently, even if unfairly, the reputation of Marxism itself as a thought-framework was at a nadir. J. C. Nyíri's joke, recounted in the introduction, simply affirmed what was the reality in a particularly striking and disquieting way—like all good jokes.

In Nyíri's Hungary, the dissolution of the "bygone era," as I have called it, was no doubt further and more overtly advanced among both philosophers and the general public than in most other parts of Eastern Europe. The probable major exception was Yugoslavia, where the contours of the "era" itself had been quite different almost from the beginning. Nevertheless, after having made all due allowances for particular national differences, I can only reaffirm the generalization that the most profound cynicism prevailed everywhere.

This being so, it may be thought almost platitudinous to say that the changes that *seemed* so sudden and dramatic when they finally occurred had been prepared for by a number of prior developments and had even, in principle (!), been predictable in general outline, although virtually no one actually did predict them in any but the vaguest way. But if we were to accept this after-the-fact judgment of predictability in its strong, literal sense, then we would be committing ourselves to the very notion of historical inevitability—albeit attributing a very different putative *content* to world history—that was one of official Marxism-Leninism's cornerstones and no doubt lingered as a probabilistic belief in many people's minds long after they had repudiated most of the rest of its thought-system. And so, although cynicism was sapping the strength of the ideological fortifications, it was still, until the end, accompanied by a shoulder-shrugging attitude of "Que faire?" that was reinforced concretely by large numbers of police, secret police, and troops, including the powerful Soviet Army. This kind of "Que faire?" implied passivity in the face of seeming ineluctability, apparent destiny—paradoxically, the very opposite implication to that of Lenin's activist *What Is To Be Done?* in his pamphlet by that title.[21] We shall return later to this philosophical issue of the meaning of history and in particular its supposed inevitability.

The wonder that should be occasioned in us as we mentally survey the ruins of this entire era in a very large and prominent area of our globe is comparable to that of Gibbon as he surveyed the ruins of the Roman Forum. The time period in question here is much shorter, of course, than that of the Roman Empire, and proportionately even much shorter is our distance from the era in question. But our wonder should be even greater than Gibbon's, I think, by virtue of the fact that we—I myself and all of the early readers of this book—lived through at least a portion of the period in question. We *remember*, most of us, when the intellectual attitudes and postures to which I have just alluded were still in effect. We remember, for instance, the vast industry—extending far beyond traditional academic institutions to encompass numerous government agencies and private or semi-private think-tanks—that was Sovietology. We remember the sometimes romance-tinged drama—for instance, the spy novels—as well as the pervasive fear and the pervasive drabness that were all parts of the Cold War. We can find vast numbers of books and articles published up to just a few years ago that take for granted large sets of assumptions about the politics and culture of Eastern Europe and that now mean even less, in some instances, than books about the same topic published a half-century or a century ago. Most important for my purposes in the remainder of this book, we can find many a philosophical treatise from between ten and fifty years ago that unwittingly betrays philosophy's inherent ambivalence as to whether (1) absolute claims about allegedly eternal truths are being made, or (2) just another story is being told to fill in our perpetual global conversation and thus alleviate our boredom. Such treatises simply *assume* the importance of certain questions and facts prominent in the bygone era that now seem as passé as the older assumptions that no black swans exist or that the other side of the moon is invisible to us. The very vocabulary of these treatises seems quaint and antiquated. Virtually *everything*, I suggest, needs to be rethought in light of the abrupt creation of these extensive ruins.

Notes

1. "Hence poetry is something more philosophic and of graver import than history, since its statements are rather of the nature of universals, whereas those of history are singulars" (Aristotle, *Poetics* 1451b). From *The Complete Works of Aristotle*, ed. J. Barnes, trans. I. Bywater, vol. 2 (Princeton: Princeton University Press).

2. Note that *Geschichte*, in Marx and Engels's native German, can be used for both "history" and "story" in English. The English usage tends, somewhat paradoxically, I think, more than the German, to absolutize "history" as humanity's super story. But that is another story. (*Das ist eine andere Geschichte.*)

3. Georg Lukács, *History and Class-Consciousness*, trans. R. Livingstone (Cambridge: MIT Press, 1971).

4. Karl Korsch, *Marxism and Philosophy*, with an introduction by Fred Halliday (New York: Monthly Review Press, 1971).

5. "[Communism] is the solution of the riddle of history and knows itself to be this solution." From a manuscript by Marx entitled "Private Property and Communism," in *Early Writings*, ed. and trans. T. B. Bottomore (New York: McGraw-Hill, 1964), 155.

6. Engels himself spoke of the "catechism form" of his draft, which I have caricatured here. It consisted of twenty-five questions and answers. See Franz Mehring, *Karl Marx: The Story of His Life*, trans. E. Fitzgerald (Ann Arbor: University of Michigan Press, 1962), 147.

7. Y. A. Kharin, *Fundamentals of Dialectics*, trans. K. Kostrov (New York: Progress, 1981).

8. William L. McBride, review of *Fundamentals of Dialectics*, by Y. A. Kharin, *Teaching Philosophy* 6, no. 2 (1983): 172.

9. Sidney Hook, *From Hegel to Marx: Studies in the Intellectual Development of Karl Marx* (1936; New York: Humanities Press, 1950). A useful recent study of this period is a book by Christopher Phelps, *The Young Sidney Hook: Marxist and Pragmatist* (Ithaca, N.Y.: Cornell University Press, 1997).

10. Gustav Wetter, *Sowjetideologie heute* (Frankfurt-am-Main: Fischer Bücherei, 1962); Innocentius M. Bochenski, *Der sowjetrussische dialektische Materialismus (Diamat)*, 2d ed. (Bern: Francke, 1962).

11. This story, together with the story of its effect in immediately altering what Polish Communist intellectuals were expected to regard as "true" and "false" in this domain, is told by Leszek Kołakowski (who attended the meeting that he describes) in "Permanent vs. Transitory Aspects of Marxism," in *Toward a Marxist Humanism: Essays on the Left Today*, trans. J. Z. Peel (New York: Grove, 1968), 173.

12. For instance, in *Western Marxism: A Critical Reader*, ed. New Left Review (London: Verso, 1978), the first two (of nine) articles dealt with Lukács.

13. See my discussion of "praxis" in the *Encyclopedia of Ethics*, ed. L. C. Becker and C. B. Becker (New York: Garland, 1992), 1005.

14. *Praxis* was published between 1964 and 1975. *Praxis International*, its successor, quite different in character but named in honor of the original, was published in Great Britain from 1981 until its dissolution, in large measure as an indirect result of the events in former Yugoslavia, in 1993. Some of those responsible for the publication of the latter now publish the journal *Constellations*, which is, once again, quite different from its predecessor. A brief account of the history of the *Praxis* group was prepared by Mihailo Marković and presented in his absence by Natalija Mićunović at a special session of the American Philosophical Association, sponsored by its Committee on International Cooperation, at the annual eastern division meetings in Boston, December 1990.

15. Well-known books by Hannah Arendt and Carl Friedrich on the topic of totalitarianism helped to codify the expression and enforce the common Western Cold War identification, from a formal point of view, of Nazism with Communism. This is not very helpful from a historical standpoint, although efforts

to continue this practice are still being made. From a philosophical standpoint, Sartre's distinction, made in his *Critique of Dialectical Reason*, between "totalizations" (ongoing, fluid) and "totalities" (rigid, fixed) seems to me to pave the way for a more nuanced conception of the sociopolitical systems envisaged under this label.

16. A very widely read early anthology of essays by Yugoslav, Czech, Polish, and other writers that reflects some of this spirit, at least as a pious hope, was *Socialist Humanism: An International Symposium*, ed. E. Fromm (New York: Doubleday, 1965).

17. It is important to note that the center was, and now once again is, the site of seminars on a wide variety of topics in the physical and social sciences and in the practice professions as well as in "philosophy" broadly understood.

18. *Hegel's Philosophy of Right*, trans. T. M. Knox (Oxford: Clarendon, 1942), 11.

19. Milovan Djilas, *The New Class: An Analysis of the Communist System* (New York: Frederick A. Praeger, 1957).

20. "Die Lüge wird zur Weltordnung gemacht."—"Three Parables," from *The Castle*, in *Existentialism from Dostoevsky to Sartre*, ed. W. Kaufmann, exp. ed. (New York: New American Library, 1975), 151. Kaufmann, p. 141, strongly objects to the English translation of this famous sentence, the force of which is indeed stronger in the German original.

21. V. I. Lenin, *What Is to Be Done?* (Oxford: Clarendon, 1963). Before Lenin, the same title had also been used by Chernyshevsky and Tolstoy.

Chapter Two

Today

What "today" means, of course, is thoroughly ambiguous. Many of the greatest philosophers—Plato, Augustine, Hegel, Sartre, and numerous others—have undertaken interesting explorations of the aporias of temporality. "Today" or "now" names, at best, a mathematical point, the reference of which shifts in the fraction of time required to speak the word. But these philosophical truisms may at certain times have seemed abstract and remote from everyday experience. In the current context of Eastern Europe, at least at certain levels of experience including the *economic*, the *political*, and the *ideological* (taking this last word for the time being in a neutral sense, one not dependent on any particular theoretical tradition), they express the lived reality. For in that reality, it often appears, there are few fixed referents and virtually everything is in flux.

Danas is the word for "today" in Serbo-Croatian (or, as the nationalists would have it, in both Serbian and Croatian) and was once the name of a leading Zagreb newsmagazine, which is mentioned in a footnote in the introduction. It died, the victim of zealots who insisted that it was not sufficiently biased toward the Croat cause. But it may be resurrected, either in something like its old form or along new lines (but who knows which?), by the time this is published, or perhaps a week from now. Let us take it as a symbol.[1]

The Economic

In my references to the recent past, the "bygone era," in chapter 1, I generally avoided discussing the *material* conditions of daily life in the diverse lands of Eastern Europe up to 1989, restricting my attention, on the whole, to the dominant philosophy and to a few of the political features. But in this chapter I find the economic domain to be the most reasonable point at which to begin this admittedly one-sided and partial survey of the state of affairs "today." Why the most reasonable? First of all, it is the closest of the three levels of experience that I have chosen to emphasize—economic, political, and ideological—to the lives of virtually everyone in the societies in question; in other words, the lived experiences of the vast majority of people in Eastern Europe, as elsewhere in our world, are thoroughly affected by economic conditions, whereas *most* changes in political regimes as such have direct consequences for far fewer, and even fewer still (though more than some intellectuals realize) are actively engaged in ideological discourses. It should be noted that this observation, while, if correct, furnishes some justification for my starting with economic conditions here, does not provide a completely compelling justification. There is, of course, no logical necessity for focusing on what affects the largest number of people simply because it is the largest number. In a different, more global context, the provinciality of most American social and political philosophy and mass media alike, which typically take as their main referent a society, their own, of a little more than a quarter billion individuals within a world population of several billion, demonstrates this point about the ultimate irrelevance of numbers all the time: the principle of "majority rule" is decisive even with seemingly ardent democrats only in those contexts in which they choose to make it so.

A second, more compelling reason for my beginning this chapter with economic phenomena is my simple judgment, shared by a great many observers with whom I have little else in common, that it is phenomena in this domain that are exerting a fundamental influence over much of the rest of what is happening in Eastern Europe today, to a greater extent than was the case under the anciens régimes.[2] Most standard formulations of Marxist theory as taught under those regimes had insisted on the base/superstructure model,[3] according to which it is the configuration of the economic base, the so-called forces of production, which manifest a certain level of industrial, technological development in a given society at a given time, that accounts for (or "causes") both the "relations of production" (that is, the property rules and other rules that govern the ways in which the forces of production are organized and utilized) and ultimately also the political superstructure and the "ideological" (ethical, philosophical, religious, etc.) codes that are designed to explain and generally to justify those rules and that superstructure. Critics of this aspect of Marxist "orthodoxy" were constantly pointing out that in fact a unilateral causality from base to superstructure obtained neither in capitalist societies nor, certainly, in the self-styled "actually existing socialist"[4] countries, where in reality the configuration of economic forces was patently influenced by ideology-driven policy considerations. In response to this sort of criticism, Marxist proponents of the base/superstructure model evolved such qualificatory formulas as Althusser's famous "determination [of superstructure by base] in the last instance."[5] Now that this entire worldview is so much out of fashion, especially in Eastern Europe, the base/superstructure model finally appears to offer, at least broadly and superficially speaking, a more or less veridical picture of the current state of affairs there!

Assurances are constantly being offered that the processes of "privatization" of both the means of production and ordinary real property, along with fiscal reform and other radical shifts in economic structure along lines designed to make East European societies more like Western ones and their inhabitants committed capitalists in ideology if not (for obvious reasons stemming from the competition-driven nature of the capitalist system itself) in fact, will in the long run bring unprecedented prosperity. In other words, "Capitalism—The Radiant Future of Mankind"[6] has become the implicit new slogan. Citizens are exhorted to bear sacrifices in the present for the sake of the society of the future. In the long run, in fact, we will all be dead (some of us, in the intermediate run). Old-age pensioners in particular have the highest statistical probability of dying fairly soon, and it is this group that is mentioned again and again, in country after country, as suffering grievously from the insecurities and downright poverty induced by situations of rapid inflation presided over by penniless governments that are being encouraged, by Western economics "experts," to regard "noninterference" in people's lives as a major virtue. In other words, the smaller the pensions relative to the actual value of the currency, the less interference there will be in the pensioners' freedom to choose between scrounging for food, clothing, and shelter, on the one hand, and starving, on the other. Like the base/superstructure model, then, the old, formerly somewhat discounted Marxist claim that capitalism has devastatingly oppressive effects on the weakest segments of society is being resurrected and validated daily in post-Communist Eastern Europe.

Privatization has had "liberating" effects on other segments of the East European populations as well. The removal or reduction of job security, along with the increased emphasis on the virtues of efficiency, has resulted in very high rates of unemployment among those of working age, particularly young adults. Many sinecures have been eliminated. So have positions in inefficient industries that have been forced to shut down. At the same time, of course, opportunities have opened up for entrepreneurs to start businesses of varying sizes. The proliferation of private kiosks, sometimes nothing more than card tables, bearing a few consumer goods such as candies and liquors, was a remarkable phenomenon in many cities in the eastern half of the European Continent, particularly during the early period of privatization. Stores with a wider range of goods have expanded their offerings or have sprung up in new sites, and restaurants have multiplied. Those who can afford to buy have options unimagined only a few years ago.

The combination of destabilization in people's lives and expectations, lower living standards for many (whether for a minority or a majority of the population does not matter in this respect, as long as it is a sizable group of people about which this can be said), and increased opportunities for spending money if one has any (and there are almost always some people who do) has had a predictable consequence: a large increase in crime rates, particularly in crimes of theft. This much is publicly known and is obvious to everyone. But it would be a neglect of philosophical responsibility to move on to other matters without at this point pausing to note the somewhat problematic character of at least two elements in my seemingly unexceptionable and commonplace observation above: the element of "predictability" and that of "theft" considered as a "crime."

To take it entirely for granted that the combination of circumstances enumerated above will *necessarily* (i.e., "with utter predictability") result in increased crime, as many journalists and sociologists do, is implicitly to reject the hypothesis of human freedom and accept a view of human nature as inherently evil (because the notion of "evil" is built into the concept of "crime"). But it seems intuitively obvious that (1) some, indeed many, East Europeans who are in very dire circumstances today have nevertheless *not* indulged in crime and that (2) at least some of these individuals have not been motivated, in this regard, solely by fear of being caught and suffering punishment. From a conceptual standpoint, there is no reason in principle why, if this is true of some or even of just one, it could not be true of more. In that case it seems to me that the hypothesis of strong determinism, which was rightly attributed to hard-line Marxist-Leninists in their day but is also attributable to hard-line advocates of the "capitalist" view that virtually all significant human behavior is motivated by economic self-interest, cannot reasonably be maintained: other factors besides some mechanical necessity for human beings in circumstances x always to act in ways $a \ldots n$ must be at work in the current situation. Among these factors are the absence, in many individuals, of any set of moral standards that would militate against their committing crimes. Another related but distinct factor is disagreement as to whether theft, at least of certain types—just which types being also a matter of dispute—should in fact be considered a crime.

"Crime," it must not be forgotten, is both a moral and a legal concept. What is defined as a crime in law is not always considered morally wrong by all of the law's subjects, and what some of those subjects consider criminally immoral is not always illegal. Moreover, in the societies in question there existed until recently an official viewpoint—to call it a mere "fiction" is both to oversimplify the actual state of affairs that obtained and to close our eyes to the importance of fictions in our lives—to the effect that the road toward a communist society was being pursued, a society of abundance in which the means of production, and much else of value besides, would be the property of the people as a whole after the State had "withered away." Furthermore, rights to legal ownership of goods not central to industrial production, even to ownership of homes and apartments, were in these societies often vested, though with different nuances of degree and kind from one place to another, in the existing, supposedly "popular," state. But there does seem, superficially at least, to be a difference in culpability between taking what is unqualifiedly the possession of someone else and taking something in which one has a theoretical share of the common ownership. Even though it was of course universally defined as a crime from a legal point of view, the taking of state property, especially in small amounts and when not intimately connected with the private life of some fellow citizen, in a "socialist" country on the road to communism could arguably be regarded as morally trivial.

The situation today is one in which, amid conditions of widespread economic displacement and impoverishment, the attempt is being made simultaneously to impose capitalist concepts, both legal and moral, of *private* property and to encourage unlimited entrepreneurship, often in the absence of new regulatory arrangements to correspond to these new concepts. The result, particularly in the extreme case of Russia, is that the line between large-scale theft and the limits of permissible profit taking is sometimes blurred and in any case exceedingly vague. The words "business" and "mafia" are not uncommonly used in combination, where "mafia" refers to extortionate practices by organized entrepreneurs rather than any Sicilian connection. Often enough, among the prominent members of the new capitalist class in countries such as Poland and the Czech Republic, there are "refugees" from the former Communist *nomenklatura* who have found it opportune and personally enriching to proclaim their dramatic conversions from Marxism-Leninism to fervent capitalist thinking. As for home ownership, the changes have resulted in the abolition of certain antecedent rights and a consequent flood of legal actions, in such countries as Hungary, Bulgaria, and above all the former East Germany, seeking to restore some real estate to its previous owners from forty-five years earlier or, more frequently for obvious reasons, to their heirs.

It would almost seem as if such developments had been planned, by someone, to maximize cynicism and skepticism about the legitimacy of private property ownership to a degree exceeding anything to be found in the writings of Marx himself. He, after all, declared in two famous companion passages in *Capital*, which have generated an extensive literature in the West on the topic of his concept of justice, that the content of rules governing economic transactions is just whenever that content is appropriate to a given mode of production, and hence the exploitation of workers who have agreed to a contract, in contrast to slavery or fraud, does not count as "unjust" under capitalism.[7] He assumed that the line between fraud and legitimate contract would always be in principle indisputable within the legal framework of a given capitalist system. But in the actual societies that we are examining, it is not always so simple as that. (He also assumed that the exploitation of workers would end in societies that considered themselves socialist. Marx was, in short, very naive.)

Nor, of course, is the legitimacy of private property itself, particularly the ownership of major tracts of land and of major manufacturing and service industries, to be taken for granted philosophically, even if it is so regarded by today's "conventional wisdom." This latter expression is apt. Property arrangements are indeed matters of convention, as the predominant thrust of Western political philosophy concerning this topic has generally asserted throughout most of its history, and "legitimacy" is at best a dubious concept when it is taken to mean anything more than "validity within a given system of conventional rules."[8] At a time when slavery had just been abolished as an outcome of the Civil War in the United States, Marx predicted, with some temerity, that the ownership of portions of the earth by single individuals would someday seem as absurd as the ownership of one human being by another already did then, according to him.[9] In a similar spirit, it needs to be observed that (1) private ownership of the "means of production," to use Marx's term, was illegal and was *considered* illegitimate under the anciens régimes in Eastern Europe and that (2) the current prevalence of a strongly contrary view that maintains, at least implicitly and sometimes explicitly, that private ownership is somehow more "natural" is no proof either of the moral superiority of this current view or of its long-term durability. The most plausible arguments in support of private property ownership, it seems to me, are arguments contending that it is more convenient and/or more generative of wealth than alternative arrangements such as the various past and possible future forms of socialism; and in much of Eastern Europe today such arguments bump up against completely opposite perceptions of economic reality that are held by large, impoverished segments of the population.

What can, I think, be said above all, by way of generalizing, as far as the economic domain is concerned, about the situation in Eastern Europe "today," despite widespread and apparently growing differences in living standards between different regions, is that that domain is topic A to a far greater extent than it was under the old regimes. Both the widespread lack of money and of what it buys and the new possibilities for making money feed into an atmosphere in which Marx's famous, once-colorful way of characterizing the real religion of capitalism, namely the "fetishism of commodities," now seems a rather pale descriptor. The structure of Marx's entire world outlook, despite interpretations to the contrary based above all on the fact that the bulk of his "mature" serious writings was devoted to economic analysis and critique, was premised on his expectation that a future society in which economic factors could be replaced by cultural concerns in the foreground of people's consciousness was a real possibility.[10] The situation of today's Eastern Europe makes such a possibility seem increasingly remote. Commodities of all price ranges dominate a world in which virtually everyone has access to a television screen on which the abundance of riches in the hands of some people is visible on a daily basis, even though most of the viewers are at present incapable of sharing in that abundance. But they can readily imagine such possession, and they know that with a certain quantity of money they would be able to achieve it. To be a major participant in the circulation process of money and commodities becomes, quite often, life's principal objective. Meanwhile, absent such participation, there remains, for all but the very poorest and least resourceful, the alternative of attempting to find solace through drugs or, more traditionally, alcohol. The statistics on increased liquor consumption (even in the midst of impoverishment) in Russia, for example, as well as in the currently much more prosperous case of Poland, have been quite overwhelming.

The Political

If there is to be a change for the better in the economic domain (and numerous economic indicators show a general decline in productivity, employment rates, and well-being for many segments of Eastern European populations since 1989) then there is only one conceivable route to achieving it, namely, through policy decisions, that is, through *political* actions. To say this, however, is to add new dimensions of irony to the present account, beyond what I have already noted in discussing the economic domain. For both Marxism-Leninism and free market capitalism are committed to reducing the role of government in theory while augmenting it in practice. In the case of Marxism-Leninism, this was actually articulated with utter candor by Stalin in a famous remark of the 1930s, the Soviet Union's decade of utmost terror, when he admitted that his version of Marxism was dedicated both to the withering away of the State and to the maximizing of Soviet state power with a view eventually to achieving this withering away, and added that this obvious contradiction was in full accordance with the principles of dialectics.[11] In the case of free market capitalist ideology, I know of no similar formula that encapsulates the reality, since this ideology's historical origins lie in the movement to abolish early modern mercantilist policies that required state intervention, and its army of contemporary proponents constantly revert to such slogans as Get Government Off Our Backs!, All Power to the Market!,[12] and similar edifying and intellectually illuminating sentiments.

If *the market* were in fact as omniscient and omnipotent as its cultists pretend, it could and of course would establish its hegemony without any serious or lasting opposition. But, in order to work, market mechanisms need to be *imposed* on sectors of daily life wherever they are not already in place, and only governments have the monopoly of power necessary to achieve or enforce such imposition. This is effected by such means as control of the money supply, manipulation of interest rates through central banks, encouragement or dissolution of monopolies as the occasion is thought to demand, selective taxation, selling off of preexisting assets to private interests (an especially salient phenomenon in the recent history of Eastern Europe), military adventures, and so on. Ronald Reagan, who preached nothing but pro-free market disengagement of government,[13] used state power to drive his country deeply into debt in order to promote a massive military buildup of enormously expensive equipment, thus arguably contributing the final exigency to bankrupt the already dreadfully decaying Soviet and (closely connected) East European economic systems as their governments sought to produce adequate counterforces. In Chile, after international business interests with strong support from the U. S. government succeeded in destabilizing the regime of Salvador Allende in 1973 and effecting the physical liquidation of him and of many of his followers, the "Chicago boys" (as they are still known in Chile and elsewhere), led by one of the most prominent free market ideologists, Milton Friedman, then of the University of Chicago, were invited by the dictator, Pinochet, to implement a forced imposition of free market mechanisms even in areas such as higher education that had been left relatively untouched by such mechanisms in other capitalist countries at the time. In the early days of cheerful "privatization" in Poland, Russia, and elsewhere in Eastern Europe after 1989, the name of Friedman and the memory of the brutal

Pinochet regime were frequently invoked in a positive way. Poland, together with, eventually, virtually all the other countries of Eastern Europe, later witnessed an electoral defeat of free market extremists. By the time of the October counterrevolution in Russia in 1993, even some right-wing Western politicians, journalists, and business leaders were beginning to express qualms about the disruptive effects of hasty privatization, or attempted privatization, there.[14] What I wish to stress here is the central role of politics in all of these developments: the right-wing libertarian anarchist vision of a pure free market society without government, or even the Night Watchman State quasi-anarchist libertarianism of a writer like Nozick,[15] is pure illusion, with no basis in reality.

The domain of politics in today's Eastern Europe is nothing if not bizarre. (This may in fact be said about the domain of politics virtually worldwide, but I shall not insist on this here!) Parties and leaders appear and disappear, often with great alacrity. In former Yugoslavia, during the heady pre-civil war days when the monopoly of the League of Communists in each of the federated republics was relaxed to allow for a multiplicity of parties, there were at one time more than one hundred serious parties in the country as a whole, distinguished among ethnic, religious, ideological, and other lines as well as by individual republic. In Bulgaria, by contrast, there was at one point something approaching a two-party system, with the socialists or reform communists being opposed by a united front of opposition groups, and the small party representing the country's Turkish minority holding the balance of parliamentary power; soon, of course, the united front disintegrated. Experimentation is obviously required, given the nearly unanimous rejection of previous political arrangements. But it is taking place, as I have already noted, against a background of economic problems of the most serious and urgent sort. Today's national hero (e.g., Václav Havel) may find himself not only out of favor with much of his former constituency tomorrow, but also presiding over the dismantling of his nation. The serious task of constitution writing, to which some very dedicated and intelligent people have devoted untold numbers of hours in the countries in question, is often overshadowed or supplanted by maneuvers undertaken by rival groups, working under old rules still in effect, that are designed to undermine the entire process; the situation of Russia in the months prior to the October 1993 events is a good example.

The relative fortunes of two prominent and contested words, "communism" and "democracy," can be seen as indicators of the complex political situation in the Eastern Europe of "today." In fact, immediately after the events of 1989, the dominant rhetoric was clear: communism was bad, democracy good. By now, this sense of apparent clarity no longer prevails. To many, "communism" is a broad term that is meant to include socialism in general and indeed any set of institutions that fails to give the broadest possible latitude to free market capitalism. To others, it means the Communist Party as it exercised its hegemony prior to 1989. The two meanings are by no means identical. There are those, of course, who long for a return to the bygone era, but in fact there are very few who believe it possible to unmake history and return to the *status quo ante*; such an expectation would indeed be utterly deluded, as well as obviously undesirable. However, a restoration of some of that era's least attractive features—its repression of dissent and insistence on adherence to a single worldview—is a distinct possibility in some, perhaps a number, of the countries of the area.

Signs of such a renaissance of repression have certainly appeared, for example, in the two largest components of former Yugoslavia, Croatia and Serbia, where on the whole, during the bygone era, the degree of insistence on conformity with the "party line" had been somewhat lower than in the countries of the Soviet Bloc. An especially poignant protest against such tendencies is to be found in a brief statement, "Je reconnais" (I acknowledge), written by one of the principal figures of the old *Praxis* group, Gajo Petrović, imitating the confessional style of self-criticism imposed on convicted victims of purge trials under the anciens régimes. Writing virtually on the eve of his impending death from a long-standing illness, he called attention to attacks in Croatian newspapers and philosophical journals that have "mentioned my name—in general, in the same manner as was done in the course of the past four decades."[16] The easiest and most frequently used way of condemning those who, like Petrović, fail to show immediate, unthinking enthusiasm for the attitudes and policies of the new regimes is to brand them as "communists."

Is this way of acting democratic? Some East European politicians, encouraging persecution of opponents through the manipulation of public opinion organs and sometimes of the legal system, would have us believe so. After all, they point out, their opponents are communists and fascists (often treated as one and the same thing), anyway, and once in power they would suppress dissenters, so that one need not be too scrupulous about niceties with respect to them. Wrapping oneself in the mantle of "democracy" has been considered de rigueur for many politicians and writers in the countries of the East (as it is, of course, for almost all politicians in the West as well), especially since any other overt stance would inevitably eliminate all possibility of support or even of toleration of one's policies and/or ideas by Western powers. Even the most bitter opponents of Yeltsin tended to proclaim themselves the true democrats, or even "Liberal Democrats" (the name of a right-wing party in Russia), as did Yeltsin himself. Granted, there are indeed outstanding individuals, including some of those most violently persecuted by today's "new democrats" of Eastern Europe, whose conception of a good political order truly is of one that "in the administration . . . hath respect not to a few but to the multitude" (to cite Pericles' definition of democracy in his famous funeral oration as translated by Hobbes, himself no lover of democracy).[17] But it must not be forgotten (and I am sure that it is not forgotten by many ordinary people) that the old regimes' self-descriptions had also strongly emphasized their allegedly democratic qualities, as in "German Democratic Republic." It was very significant, along the same lines, that the first regular article of the first issue of the Bulgarian philosophy journal *Filosofska Misul* in 1945 was an analysis of "The Scientific Concept of Democracy and Certain Questions of Our Time."[18] Thus the past history of the rhetoric, including the philosophical rhetoric, about democracy reinforces a widespread attitude of skepticism about many of today's most enthusiastic self-proclaimed democrats. As well it should.

But the skepticism that, as I perceive it, is virtually all-pervasive in the domain of politics in today's Eastern Europe extends well beyond the multitudinous and often incompatible proclamations of allegiance to democracy: it encompasses the entire profession and practice of politics as such. True, this is more or less a worldwide phenomenon, occurring in the United States, Western Europe, Africa, Japan, and other places as well. But it has attained a certain apogee in the countries in question, where public opinion polls, low voter turnout figures, the general level of criticism in the newly liberated press, and many other signs point to a widespread feeling of disillusionment and apathy. As much as politicians of the free market democrat sort strive, like Communist politicians before them, to use the machinery of the state to reshape society in accordance with their ideological commitments while "earnestly" (more or less) reaffirming an ultimately antistate posture in the long run, great numbers of nonpoliticians try as much as they can to avoid having to do with the state and its politicians here and now. One very popular conceptual tool for abetting this antistate attitude, particularly in the months immediately preceding and following the cataclysmic changes of 1989, was the notion of "civil society."

This concept, prominent in the writings of Locke, Hegel, and Marx, among others, but bearing quite different normative weights in each, was treated very positively in a number of the writings of that early period, although today it has already receded somewhat in prominence. Roughly speaking, civil society is that aspect of everyday life in which citizens act together, in small or large voluntary associations, apart from the self-aggrandizing state or government. It was this sphere, so it was contended, that the Communist state had succeeded in large measure in destroying: the totalitarian state is by definition all-encompassing, and an independent civil society would constitute an obstacle to it. The task, then, was to reconstruct civil society in all its multifariousness, its plurality, its independence. Writers associated with Solidarnosc, the Polish party that had been regarded as a beacon of hope for change in the 1980s, that served as the vehicle for Lech Walesa's rise to power, and that was eventually repudiated by him and reduced to electoral insignificance, were among those who emphasized the positive valence of civil society.

Whether civil society has in fact been reconstructed in such a way as to substitute, positively, for the demands and intrusions into people's lives that were features of the former Communist state apparatuses is a question that admits a variety of answers, depending both on one's appraisal of the current state of affairs (which will obviously vary greatly both from one country to another and from one appraiser to another) and on one's understanding of "civil society." Before undertaking an appraisal of the present in this regard, one must first become clear as to just *how* "totalitarian," by comparison, the various anciens régimes actually were, and also as to whether one wishes to regard all of their initiatives in such diverse areas as culture and housing construction as entirely negative. It is obvious that, unlike Plato's ideal statesman who would "sit beside" his subjects to guide them on an hourly basis, the "totalitarian" nature of those regimes was not absolutely total; otherwise, all dissident activity and many ordinary, nonpolitical activities of ordinary people would have been utterly impossible. And it is equally clear, or clearer, that much was achieved of a positive sort by those regimes, the former Soviet Union's promotion of the classical ballet being a good example,[19] even though to say this is not to preclude even severe criticism of some aspects of these same achievements (e.g., the comparative downgrading of contemporary ballet). Only after having taken account of these considerations, I think, is one in a position to reasonably assess the comparative quality of life in Eastern Europe "today" and formulate some judgments. That part of ordinary life that in a flourishing society consists of cultural activities is one about which considerable debate is possible with respect to the current situation. The widespread reduction or elimination of state subsidies for the more costly of these activities (e.g., ballets, orchestras, theatres, etc.) in the post-Communist era, for example, has occasioned considerable concern.[20] Whether or not such concern has validity (and again, as in all these matters, there are great differences from one country to another and often from one month to the next in the same country), one can also ask whether cultural activities are truly central to the life of civil society, anyway. And that returns us to the question of what is meant by "civil society."

The importance of this issue, I would like to stress, comes from the fact that the idea of a dynamic civil society was, and often still is, treated as a major criterion for identifying new possibilities for people's lives to be made available under the new dispensation, possibilities that could serve as substitutes for (or at least complements to) the more strictly political activities that had allegedly been all-encompassing in the bygone era. Thus, clarity as to the nature of this presumably renascent domain of human existence, civil society, becomes crucial. But the classical philosophical literature in which the expression was originally formulated offers somewhat confusing guidance, as would any effort to extract an univocal meaning from the contemporary multidisciplinary literature on the topic that fills our library shelves.[21] For Locke, whom history-conscious Eastern Europeans seeking to supplant Marxian with liberal democratic thoughtways may rightly regard as an important distant ancestor, "civil or political society" (taken as equivalent terms) was contrasted with the quasi-mythical state of nature and regarded as the solid base, as it were, out of which government was generated; this base could very well perdure, as far as Locke was concerned, across even revolutionary changes in government without any necessary relapse into a state of nature. But Locke, I think it fair to say, says very little about the concrete content of civil society as he understands it. For Hegel, civil society, *bürgerliche Gesellschaft*, names the domain above all of economic activity (i.e., of need satisfaction) and of much that is connected therewith—the market, business organizations, criminal and civil law, the police, as well as contrasts of wealth and poverty. It constitutes (as it did for Locke) a level in society beyond that of the family or tribe, but it risks arbitrariness and the irrational favoring of certain particular interests over common interests unless subjected to the control of the higher, more universally oriented level that is the state. Marx, strongly influenced by Hegel but unimpressed by the latter's very positive, synthetic view of his own contemporary world order, saw *bürgerliche Gesellschaft*, "*bourgeois* society" in another translation, as in fact dominant over both individuals and the state under capitalism and hence as the key to explaining the contradictions and *failings* of this system.[22] It was said that Marx virtually spat with contempt when he pronounced the term in German.

Thus any appeal to civil society as a panacea does indeed constitute a direct challenge to Marx's worldview, if one stresses the history of the expression. However, this may not help a great deal in assessing either the healthiness of the political climate or the quality of daily life in Eastern Europe today. As many a punster has remarked, there is much about that life, lived as it is under conditions of decreasing standards of living for many and in the absence of much by way of common objectives (for which truly respected political leaderships, if there could be any such, could serve as a focus) and the presence of strong incentives exclusively to pursue private profit if one is able, that is very *uncivil*. And so, given this actual state of affairs and the extreme polyvalence of the term itself, it is doubtful whether the appeal to civil society over against the state, the bureaucracy, and the politicians, though it remains strategically important in the development of new ways of thinking and speaking, can regain the incantatory charm that it had only a few years ago.

The Ideological

In the preceding discussions of the economic and political (and/or antipolitical) domains in today's Eastern Europe, allusions to related ideological positions have, of necessity, arisen constantly, as my treatment of civil society has well illustrated. Admittedly, to consign the range of climates of thought and worldviews to the blanket notion of the "ideological" domain is deliberately to ignore important analytic distinctions, such as those between ideology and philosophy, ideology and science, philosophy and worldview, and so on, that have considerable conceptual value (although, as in the case of civil society and related concepts, different writers have drawn the lines of distinction in different and sometimes incompatible ways). Here, however, I am concerned to try to capture and present an atmosphere, that of today's Eastern Europe, in which the lines between painstaking philosophical analyses and philosophically inspired essays directed to the general reading public, and even between the latter and political sloganizing, are often blurred in practice. (The first type of blurring, I think, is not always a bad thing, whereas the second is.) Hence I have resorted to the term "ideological," employed in a very general and for the moment nontendentious sense, to refer to the gamut of writing and thinking *about* the economic and political domains. It is a world in which, to some degree, Marx's and many Marxists' dreams of bringing theory and practice together is realized, and it is not always neat or pretty.

For Marx, to be sure, "ideology," as featured in his joint work (with Engels) *The German Ideology*, has distinctly negative connotations. He did very little in this unfinished text to make his meaning of the term more precise, and so this was left to commentators, including Soviet commentators, who (the latter group, that is) in the last analysis did not hesitate to reverse the "spin" that he had put on it. For them, "ideological work" came to mean something quite positive. Today, of course, the "ideology" that was Marxist is publicly held in low regard in Eastern Europe, at best surviving in little pockets here and there, for example, in occasional papers with almost the same aura about them that *samizdat* publications formerly had in Russia. There are still plenty of thinkers who will acknowledge, some shamefacedly and some fearlessly, a youthful Marxian influence on their own worldviews. One can readily observe a continuing influence of certain habits of thought prominent in Marxism, such as a highly historical approach to philosophy and to social phenomena, on many of those who occupy academic and other intellectual positions in the countries in question. (This is hardly surprising in view of the fact that all but the youngest of them, with the exception of East Germany because of the "colonization" process mentioned in my introduction, received their training under the ancien régime.) But in general the admission that Marx had something important and valuable to say about the world, when not taken as mere platitude, is graded along a spectrum of characterizations ranging from "not chic" to downright dangerous. This is unfortunate, first, since Marxism is possessed of some splendid resources for the critique of economic and political concepts in particular and of theoretical slogans and shibboleths in general and, second, the repressed Marx may return to East European cultural life at some unforeseeable future time(s). These two convictions of mine would not be appropriate to pursue very far here, in our discussion of the *current* situation.[23]

What, then, are some of the dominant "ideological" tendencies that have replaced Marxism in Eastern Europe today? Among them are a blend of free market capitalism with various versions of democracy; postmodernism; resurgent religious thought; and nationalism. Admixtures of all of these are conceivable, and no doubt every possible combination is subscribed to, whether plausibly or not, by someone or other.[24] Postmodernism with nationalism may seem an especially peculiar combination (one has only to think, for example, of Jacques Derrida's deconstruction of nationalism in *L'Autre Cap*),[25] but in fact I think a good argument can be made for seeing even these two trends as partners by virtue of their common opposition to universalizing assumptions about humanity that lie at the core of the so-called discourse of modernity associated with the spirit of the Enlightenment.

Concerning the blend of free market advocacy with democratic sloganizing, it is important to note, as I have already implied in my account of the state's needed role in imposing free market mechanisms, that the two things, free market and democracy, are incompatible with one another in their pure forms—a point fraught with practical implications for the Eastern Europe of today and tomorrow. The reason for this incompatibility is obvious enough. Maintenance of a truly *pure* free market requires guarantees against the retention or institution of "external" constraints on its workings, and yet it is always possible for an electorate and/or its representatives democratically to opt for such constraints, as the rejection of the most strongly pro-free market parties throughout most of Eastern Europe in the mid-1990s shows. (Indeed, this democratic opting for constraints on market "freedom" happens all the time, even in countries such as the United States in which free market ideology is particularly virulent.) In practical terms, in the contemporary world at least, the "pure" form of democracy, permanent participatory democracy, is no more realizable than is a pure free market economy; among many other reasons why this is so is that the universal awareness of background facts needed for citizens of a participatory democracy to make intelligent choices is simply inaccessible in light of the complexities of our world, to say nothing of the obstacles to clear thinking introduced by advertising and other forms of propaganda.[26] Nevertheless, in today's Eastern Europe one can still encounter pronouncements at every level, including that of professional philosophy, asserting the desirability of forging "true market democracies" in that region, in imitation of what spokespersons for the Western powers claim their own nations to be. A certain skepticism has, however, begun to set in concerning this ideological blend, especially since the efforts (often extremely quixotic, if I am correct) to realize it in practice have thus far produced, at best, mixed results—from mildly positive to catastrophic depending on the country and/or social group at which one is looking—at the level of daily life.

Whoever uses the word "skepticism" in the contemporary context ipso facto invokes postmodernism. However frustrating and self-defeating attempts to define this broad current of thought must necessarily be,[27] it surely includes, as perhaps the most important part of its agenda, a complete repudiation of the so-called grand narratives about "man" (the use of the word associated with the male half of humanity is not accidental), "society," "world," and so on, that dominated the systematic philosophies of the past, including the recent past. Among the grand narrators attacked by writers in a postmodern vein, Marx himself was often included even prior to 1989; and of course the even more clearly systematic and totalistic worldview known as "orthodox" Marxism or Marxism-Leninism fell even more obviously within the scope of this critique. An interesting argument could be made (although, like all such sweeping historical claims, it could hardly be demonstrated with certainty) to the effect that postmodern thinking, with its emphasis on intellectual "decentering," anticipated and perhaps prepared the way for the *political* decentering of Eastern Europe—and even of some of its component countries—that has taken place and is continuing to occur today. One evident direction in which such thinking can be taken, as has been pointed out many times already, is that of total disengagement and refusal to take any stand whatever. It is unnecessary, I think, to belabor the point that this implication of the thought of some (by no means of all)[28] intellectuals identified with postmodernism resonates well with the disgust with politics and related attitudes of social disengagement felt by many East Europeans, to which I have already referred.

The resurgence of religious thinking and values in Eastern Europe today is extremely varied in kind and degree of intensity. It was accompanied by great cynicism in parts of former Yugoslavia, where some leaders with no record of prior religious commitments or interest pulled their respective ethnic groups' religions about them like cloaks and then used them to promote blatant cruelties and injustices. In Poland, the Catholic Church hierarchy's obsession with the practice of abortion has created new rifts in the society and has led to a certain backlash against this institution, which once stood above all others as the rallying point for opposition to the old regime. In Hungary, the tripling or quadrupling of churchgoing in a society in which such behavior had previously been confined to a very small minority of the population still leaves churchgoers very much in the minority. Nevertheless, after all these caveats, the resurgence of interest in religious or more generally spiritual thinking, much of it not directly dependent on established ecclesiastical organizations, is palpable in many places, including Russia, Bulgaria, Slovakia, the Baltic states, and so on. Much of it is oriented toward mysticism and the spiritual quest for transcendence. In many of its adherents, it is disassociated from the exclusivism and intolerance that have so often characterized Western religions in particular. However, by virtue of its inherent conviction that what takes place in human time is not exhaustive of what is, and hence that failures in human time are not to be seen as total failures, it does have the function of somewhat mitigating the disillusionment that is so widespread today, thus demonstrating that there is some truth to Marx's metaphorical dictum that religion is the opiate of the people. One need not necessarily, however, interpret that dictum as the repudiation of religion that he obviously meant it to be. These matters are considered in more detail in chapter 6.

Nationalism is also a focus of attention in that chapter. But it is such an inescapable part of today's climate that I feel that it needs to be mentioned here, at the conclusion of my general discussion of ideology within the context of the Eastern Europe of today. Nationalism need not always assume the virulent, murderous forms that it lately assumed, particularly in former Yugoslavia and in portions of the former Soviet Union, for example. American and West European critics of the resurgent nationalisms among some of the relatively small ethnic groups in Eastern Europe might do well first to reflect on the enormously greater menace inherent in the periodically resurgent nationalism of the world's multiethnic superpower, the United States, when it is directed at some poor "third world" people or other, for example, the Iraqis, the Libyans, the Vietnamese, and so on. Nevertheless, it is difficult for the observer from outside Eastern Europe, when reflecting on today's East European nationalisms, to avoid reverting to the old myth of historical progress[29] and pontificating, on the basis of this myth, that here we see instances of obvious, though it is to be hoped temporary, retrogression. Such pontificating, widespread as it is today, points to some especially paradoxical aspects of the present situation.

On the one hand, what seems at first glance to be completely clear and unambiguous about this situation is that there has been a fundamental change, since 1989, in the ideological, as in the economic and political, climates of Eastern Europe. But then, on the other hand, it would be difficult to deny that the upsurge of nationalist sentiment is one salient manifestation or symptom of this "revolution." For the typical Western liberal imbued with the myth of progress, however, as I have pointed out, it appears equally difficult to deny that, according to the usual configurations of this myth, the resurgent nationalist element in this supposed fundamental change is more deserving of the label "counterrevolution" than "revolution." And indeed the invocation of supposed past glories and/or defeats is an important part of most nationalist movements in the regions in question. (Serb nationalists, for example, have constantly alluded to the historic defeat of the Serbian army by Turks at Kosovo six centuries ago.) One commonplace way of explaining this apparent paradox, which constitutes a salient exception to the once general, now waning Western liberal attitude of satisfaction over the events of 1989, is to say that murderous nationalist sentiments were "there" all along, just kept out of sight by the Communist totalitarians. Setting aside the considerable oversimplification and historical inaccuracy of this explanation, however, one is forced to admit that, to the degree to which it *is* accurate, a less fundamental change has in fact occurred than might at first have been thought.

As a graduate student in the 1960s, I considered possible topics on which to focus my earliest sustained philosophical reflections for my doctoral dissertation. Slogans about revolution, inspired especially though not exclusively by Marxist thought, were very much in the air, and so it seemed to me worthwhile to try to get beneath the level of sloganizing in the interest of a more serious philosophical analysis of fundamental social change, showing in detail, for example, why in this context "fundamental" could never become equivalent to "absolute."[30] Today, just a generation later,[31] we find ourselves at the other side of the Marxist or pseudo-Marxist revolutionary period, confronted with phenomena of "velvet revolutions" and with puzzling claims about a brave, radically new world "order." The slogans are different, but the need to get beneath the level of sloganizing is as great as ever.

Notes

1. The same symbolic value might be attributed, alas, to a Russian publication with a cognate name, *Den'* (Day), an extremist anti-Semitic and anti-Yeltsin newspaper that fell victim to his censorship in the wake of the failed uprising of October 1993.

2. Of course I am not claiming that economic concerns had *no* significant influence over policy and thought in the bygone era. In Poland, for example, demonstrations and strikes over officially decreed prices for food and other staple items led on several occasions to political changes, to "liberalizations," and so on. I am simply making a rather sweeping comparative judgment, and a very fallible one at that.

3. See my critical review of three Marx interpretations published in English, including perhaps the best defense of the base/superstructure model, G. A. Cohen's *Karl Marx's Theory of History: A Defence*, in "Tendencies in Marxology and Tendencies in History," *Ethics* 92, no. 2 (January 1982): 316–26.

4. This expression and its equivalents, "really existing socialism" or "real socialism," was developed originally, in the pre-1989 years, as a sort of sloganized response to socialist critics of the Eastern European regimes who pointed out how far short of one or another socialist ideal these societies fell. Well, the defenders of the regimes replied, one may talk forever about ideals, but we have really existing socialism already, even if it still exhibits some defects, and it is these regimes that socialists should support. Today the same expression is usually used ironically and negatively. Looking back at the anciens régimes, it is implied, consider what "real socialism" amounted to, and you will not give another thought to socialism as a possible future ideal.

5. Louis Althusser, *For Marx*, trans. B. Brewster (New York: Vintage, 1970), 111.

6. My allusion is to Aleksandr Zinoviev's excellent satirical work about the Soviet Union, *The Radiant Future* (London: Bodley Head, 1981).

7. The two passages are in vol. 1, chap. 7, sect. 2, and vol. 3, chap. 21. See Karl Marx, *Capital*, vol. 1, trans. S. Moore and E. Aveling, ed. F. Engels (Moscow: Foreign Languages Publishing House, 1961), 194; vol. 3, ed. F. Engels (Moscow: Foreign Languages Publishing House, 1962), 333–34. For a discussion of their meaning and of some of the relevant literature, see William L. McBride, "The Concept of Justice in Marx, Engels, and Others," *Ethics* 85, no. 3 (1975): 204–18.

An amusing anecdotal example of the clash of concepts and ideologies concerning private property, within the framework of a "national" entity supposedly on the road to socialism, that I personally witnessed occurred at a session of the annual Korčula summer school in the former "nation" of Yugoslavia during the early 1970s. An Italian participant, Luigi Lombardo-Radice, a prominent member of the Central Committee of the Italian Communist Party who was also a professor of mathematics, had driven his private automobile there, taking a ferry to bring it onto the island. There were very few automobiles on the island at the time, much less Western automobiles, and so it stood out, even though it was not a deluxe model. Some student participants presumably decided that such relatively ostentatious (in the circumstances) private possession was hypocritical and antisocialist and so proceeded to "expropriate" the car to some hidden site. When their action was discovered and the car was returned, Lombardo-Radice delivered a brief lecture on his understanding of socialism as a future ideal that did not entail personal impoverishment, but indeed the opposite.

8. For an extended skeptical analysis of the concept of "legitimacy," see William L. McBride, "The Fetishism of Illegality and the Mystifications of 'Authority' and 'Legitimacy,'" *Georgia Law Review* 18, no. 4 (1984): 863–90.

9. *Capital*, vol. 3, chap. 46, 757.

10. This point is ably defended by Louis Dupré in *Marx's Social Critique of Culture* (New Haven: Yale University Press, 1983).

11. "We are in favour of the withering away of the state, yet we are at the same time in favour of strengthening the dictatorship of the proletariat, which represents the most powerful and mighty of all forms of state power that have hitherto existed. The supreme development of the power of the state, with the object of the withering away of state power—such is the Marxist formula. Is that 'self-contradictory'? Yes, it is 'self-contradictory.' But this contradiction is a living thing, and it is a complete reflection of Marxian dialectics." Joseph Stalin, "Deviations on the National Question" [report delivered at the sixteenth congress of the CPSU, June 1930], in *Marxism and the National and Colonial Question*, trans. A. Fineberg, Marxist Library (New York: International Publishers, 1934), 261–62.

12. This latter slogan is of course a paraphrase of what is really said, but it is semantically equivalent.

13. This contrast between Reagan's rhetoric of freedom and diminution of government, on the one hand, and his actual use of very strong government to promote certain goals, on the other hand, has always reminded me of the following famous passage from Machiavelli: "[Pope] Alexander VI never did anything else, never had another thought, except to deceive men, and he always found fresh material to work on. Never was there a man more convincing in his assertions, who sealed his promises with more solemn oaths, and who observed them less. Yet his deceptions were always successful, because he knew how to manage this sort of business." Niccolò Machiavelli, *The Prince*, trans. R. M. Adams (New York: Norton, 1977), 48.

14. Even American Republican Party leaders such as Robert Dole began to publicly express such sentiments at that time.

15. Robert Nozick, *Anarchy, State, and Utopia* (New York: Basic Books, 1974).

16. Gajo Petrović, "Je reconais," *Lignes* 20 (September 1993): 154. My translation.

17. Thucydides, *The Peloponnesian War*, trans. T. Hobbes (Chicago: University of Chicago Press, 1989), 109.

18. *Filosofska Misul* 1–2 (1945): 5–55. This is mentioned in the article by W. McBride and I. Raynova, "Visions from the Ashes: Philosophical Life in Bulgaria from 1945 to 1992," in *Philosophy and Political Change in Eastern Europe*, ed. Barry Smith (LaSalle, Ill.: Monist Library of Philosophy, 1993), 107.

19. For a discussion of this, see William L. McBride, "Culture and Justice and Cultural Injustices," *Proceedings of the World Congress of Philosophy*, Montreal, 1983, published (on microfiche) as *Philosophie et Culture* (Montréal: Éditions Montmorency, 1988), 2: 208–12.

20. As an example of such concern, see Pravda Spassova, "Perspectives on Art after the Failure of Real Socialism," *Praxis International* 12, no. 2 (1992): 163–67.

21. I actually made such an effort, with results that can probably best be characterized as hilarious. See the first section of my paper "Clarifying 'Civil Society' and Creating Space for Civil Societies: From the Struggle against Nation-State Despotisms to the Critique of Despotic Transnationalisms," in *Resurrecting the Phoenix: Proceedings from the International Congress on Civil Society in South East Europe: Philosophical and Ethical Perspectives*, ed. David C. Durst, Maria Dimitrova, Alexander Gungov, and Borislava Vassileva (Sofia: EOS, 1998).

22. By (partial) contrast with all three of these classical views, the authors of a magisterial recent work on this topic, Jean L. Cohen and Andrew Arato, advocate a conception of civil society that is distinct from both economic and political domains but includes, among other things, the family. See their *Civil Society and Political Theory* (Cambridge: MIT Press, 1992).

23. See William L. McBride, "The Pathos of European Political Philosophy after Marxism," *Journal of Philosophical Research* 19 (1994): 331–43. See also Jacques Derrida, *Spectres of Marx: The State of Debt, the Work of Mourning, and the New International*, trans. P. Kamuf (New York: Routledge, 1994).

24. For instance, I am acquainted with one fairly prominent philosopher in an Eastern European country whose principal acknowledged intellectual influences are Sartre, Pope John Paul II, and Muammar Qaddafi.

25. Jacques Derrida, *The Other Heading: Reflections on Today's Europe*, trans. P.-A. Brault and M. B. Naas (Bloomington: Indiana University Press, 1992).

26. This point was already made by one of the Western tradition's foremost analysts of participatory democracy, Jean-Jacques Rousseau, who introduced his mechanism of the "legislator," the wise outsider, as a way of resolving problems stemming from the fact that the citizens' guiding judgment "is not always enlightened." An important discussion of twentieth-century develop-

ments that have made the achievement of "genuine" democracy even more unattainable and have shown the incoherence of most commonplace conceptions of democracy that are still current is Danilo Zolo, *Democracy and Complexity* (State College: Pennsylvania State University Press, 1992).

27. See William L. McBride, "Sartre and His Successors: Existential Marxism and Postmodernism at Our *Fin de Siècle*," *Praxis International* 11, no. 1 (1991): 78–92; idem, "Sartre e il postmodernismo," *segni e comprensione* 16 (1992): 21–30.

28. Only a few years ago, it was a commonplace among critics of postmodernism to say that this admittedly protean movement was hostile to any stance of political commitment. Writers attracted to postmodernism but also sympathetic to political change engaged in what appeared, to me and to many other observers, to be heroic efforts to reconcile the two things. (Feminist legal theorist Drucilla Cornell is a good example of this.) At the conference in Budva, Montenegro, that I attended in May 1991 just before the outbreak of civil war in former Yugoslavia, I recall a defense of postmodernism by one of the participants from Belgrade that treated it as encouraging an "anything goes" position more or less across the board, together with a critique of virtually all structures; although this was an extreme version, it reflected, I think, a widespread conception of the implications of postmodernism among defenders as well as critics of the time. By now, however, the cultural landscape in this respect has changed as much as the political landscape. Derrida's more recent books, cited in notes 23 and 25 above, represent two of several new directions being taken. The late Jean-François Lyotard himself, who in a way "defined" the movement more clearly than anyone else, took a somewhat new turn in his *Moralités Postmodernes* (Paris: Galilée, 1993). And Richard Rorty, whom many Europeans in particular (including the Belgrade participant to whom I have alluded) tended to regard as the most important herald of postmodernism (which thus came to be seen by some as a primarily American development, whereas I think Americans have tended to consider it European in origin and at base), has evolved in a number of directions that have brought him somewhat closer to those engaged in committed sociopolitical activities, for example, feminists.

29. I have dealt with this myth in "The Progress of Technology and the Philosophical Myth of Progress," *Philosophy and the History of Science: A Taiwanese Journal* 1, no. 1 (1992): 31–58.

30. "The limiting case of a fundamental change in law and society is an *absolute* change, after which no aspect of human life (and consequently not even human life itself) would be the same as before. But this is clearly a myth ('the myth of the new life,' to use [Henri] Lefebvre's term), though it may sometimes prove suggestive and helpful." *Fundamental Change in Law and Society*, 212.

31. Although there are some interesting and probably important philosophical issues surrounding the question of the meaning(s) of a "generation," here I simply mean something like twenty-five to thirty years.

Chapter Three

Conversions and Continuities

One of the most "wondrous," to me, of all the elements in the recent events in Eastern Europe has been the numerous instances of fundamental change in the professed commitments of philosophers, politicians, philosopher-politicians, and many others to basic principles governing their social, and hence to some extent even their individual, lives. (Indeed, during the most totalitarian moments in the history of the Eastern Bloc, the separation of individual lives from social lives was, especially for those who were most politically involved, at least in principle rather slight.) It is a remarkable experience to find a philosopher who throughout his long career wrote major, widely distributed texts supporting Marxist-Leninist dialectical materialism along with, at least by implication, the political allegiances associated with that system of thought at its height, later urging, during a period of uncertainty and transition in his own country (Russia), abandonment of the Communist Party and a rethinking of everything from the ground up—while at the same time urging his Western colleague to read one of those very texts that had contributed to his fame and reputation within the Communist system![1] We have all, of course, heard of and known individuals who have undergone dramatic "conversions" of various sorts—from irreligion to religion or the reverse, from one kind of lifestyle to another, from one close personal relationship to another, and so on; such cases are often surprising, sometimes not. But the present situation is one in which there *appears* to have been a shift of fundamental beliefs on a massive scale. The cases of intellectuals are, at least on the surface, particularly interesting in this respect, simply because they *are* thinkers, that is, persons who are supposed to be taking their professed principles very seriously. In this chapter I propose to try to get behind the appearances and explore some of the realities—rather complex, as I see them—of these developments.

The first point to be emphasized is that there exists a wide variety of individual cases and types of cases. Let me try to catalogue some of them. There are, of course, the outright opportunists, to whom the only "principle" that mattered before or matters now is the maximization of personal self-interest: for them, self-interest dictated giving unqualified support to whatever was the prevailing interpretation of Marxism-Leninism before, and now, although the fluidity of today's situation makes these shoals somewhat more difficult to navigate, self-interest requires supporting whatever ideological notions appear most central to the party in power this week. In such a stance in its purest form, questions of bad faith—of "lying to oneself" or "self-deception," as Sartre and many writers from various philosophical traditions have put it[2]—may never arise. There is, by definition, no deception, since it is simply a matter of reacting to the new direction(s) in which the wind is blowing. But such *pure*, unabashed opportunism may in fact be somewhat more difficult to attain than is often believed, especially when the individual attempting to practice it is a philosopher who must presumably provide, or at least allude to, reasons for taking any given position, in particular a position that he or she is known to have denounced a month ago.

Then, of course, there are the "authentic" individuals whose ideas and principles have remained more or less the same, and known as such, across the major political transition: those who were consistently committed to worldviews having little or nothing in common with Marx and Marxism (except perhaps by way of opposition to it), and still are; those who, as Gajo Petrović portrayed himself in his last "confession" mentioned earlier, were known as dissidents from the "official" line, or who, to use the terminology employed in the account of Bulgaria cited earlier, functioned as "marginals" but found *something* of value in Marx's thought and now continue to hold approximately the same positions (which may now still be regarded as "dissident," but in different ways from before); and lastly those, probably a fairly small number among intellectuals but still not an insignificant portion of the general population in many countries, who were profoundly accepting of orthodox Marxism-Leninism as they understood it and still remain so despite the vastly changed circumstances. The first group is of little interest for my present concerns, while the second group includes many of those whom I most admire. A serious consistency problem arises for the last group, inasmuch as the official "line" typically included an assertion of the inevitable eventual triumph of Communism in human history, whereas to continue to believe in this prediction and at the same time to maintain a hearty materialist confidence in the validity of empirical evidence, the preponderance of which is at present so greatly at odds with it, seems virtually untenable.

It would be a serious misunderstanding of almost everything about human consciousness, however, if we were to expect total logical consistency in the attitudes of *anyone*, much less in persons caught up in such traumatic and turbulent times. Granted, the simplest way of explaining fundamental changes in principled beliefs about social reality is to say that the individual in question has undergone a conversion, whether a relatively minor one requiring, for instance, the rejection of one or several significant tenets of his or her previous set of Marxist-Leninist ideas (such as the tenet of Communism's inevitable triumph) while permitting the retention of all the rest, or, on the contrary, a major conversion away from everything that was important to his or her previous way of thinking. But it seems clear to me that the latter, radical sort of conversion is a limiting case, virtually if not utterly unachievable in the actual world in which we live. Quite common, on the other hand, are attempts to make a truce with changing reality, adjustments, accepting or even cultivating ambiguities, and, yes, often enough, procedures of what must be called bad faith. I would like to argue, then, that the simplest route to explanation in fact vastly oversimplifies what has actually taken place in countless cases over the past few years in Eastern Europe. We need to explore this development in some of its real complexity.

I shall return shortly to the "limiting case" phenomenon, or alleged phenomenon, of "radical conversion." This term, like "bad faith," was employed extensively by Jean-Paul Sartre; I am using both terms here because I find them helpful in coming to grips with the "wondrous" events upon which I am focusing here. The notion of "bad faith" has become quite popular in a wide spectrum of literature and is hence very familiar even to those who may be unaware of its largely Sartrean provenance. But that provenance may furnish clues to the concept's limitations as well as to its usefulness. Sartre's own view of human consciousness, especially in his earlier writings in which bad faith is featured most prominently, was that of an operation of, at the limit, total lucidity, which could clearly grasp the choices open to itself and be reflectively aware of the grounds for its decisions. A typical Sartrean example of living in bad faith is the man who continually performs homosexual acts but denies that he is a homosexual. In a sense he is right to deny it, since human reality for Sartre is always changeable and without an essence, and the man might conceivably choose tomorrow to cease entirely from such activity henceforth and in fact stick with this decision; but in another sense he is lying to himself by refusing to acknowledge the uncomfortable truth. (Needless to say, this example comes from a time and place in which homosexuality was generally regarded as quite shameful, before the birth of "gay pride.") It is not as if, for Sartre, this individual is simply confused or "fuzzy" about his situation, at least not in principle. He is just deceiving himself out of self-interested motives and could probably be gotten, under appropriate conditions (e.g., in a therapy session with an existential psychoanalyst), to analyze the basis of his attitude and admit that it was in bad faith.

One key to understanding what is occurring in instances of bad faith, which for Sartre are so numerous as to dominate much of everyday life and indeed virtually all of some individuals' lives, is to see it as a kind of *faith*, of which religious faith is a paradigm example: Sartre calls it a "metastable" phenomenon,[3] an attitude of consciousness that includes both an element of rigidity and fixedness inasmuch as a person's faith consists in firm adherence to certain propositions, certain claims about the world, and an element of extreme fluidity, inasmuch as it can dissolve at any time.

Two of the best models, it seems to me, of "faith" of this kind are the dogmatic Catholicism that was held by some of Sartre's acquaintances in the France of his youth,[4] which I learned as a budding theology student whose knowledge of this discipline reached its height during my seventh and eighth grades of elementary school,[5] and which Pope John Paul II professed and insisted that the errant faithful should embrace anew; and, along parallel lines, the orthodox Marxism-Leninism, described in chapter 1, that was taught in "diamat" courses in Eastern Europe at the height of the ancien régime. (Some prominent contemporary versions of Islam are probably equally good models, but I am insufficiently familiar with them to be sure of this.) A dogmatic faith of this type consists of a number of propositions stating alleged truths both about reality and about what ought to be done and shunned, and the common expectation among its adherents and especially among its guardians (Sacred Congregations or chief ideologists) is that it must be accepted as a "package," an interconnected whole. It is all clear and well defined (even if, in the case of a dogmatic religion, certain questions may be treated as off-limits to ordinary analytic understanding and declared unfathomable "mysteries"), and, within the clearly defined parameters, a high level of sophisticated, systematic thought is possible. Dissolution may occur in a number of ways, for example, when the previously faithful religious believer is confronted with a situation in which what seems obviously right and desirable conflicts directly, and without a chance of evasion or "fudging," with a dogmatic moral prescription (e.g., that any premarital sexual activity or the use of contraception within marriage is always, unequivocally, a deadly sin justifying eternal damnation); or when the previously faithful party member finds the party ordering an obviously unjust imprisonment or execution; or alternatively when the believer of one or the other sort comes to feel that a certain claim within the body of dogma concerning what is real simply cannot be squared in any way with another proposition, about the truth of which he or she has independently become entirely convinced.

In light of this dogmatic type of model, it is easy to see the close relationship between faith and "bad faith." For instance, the Catholic who claims to be one of the faithful, subscribing to the dogma of papal infallibility in those matters of faith and morals that have been formally declared to be the subjects of infallible pronouncements, who agrees that "in principle" contraception is one such matter, and who nevertheless asserts that the practice of contraception in certain circumstances is morally right must, it would seem, be living in bad faith. The same could be said of the avowed Communist Party militant of recent past times who had concluded, contrary to his or her avowals, that the party's claim to be the vanguard of the proletariat was untenable nonsense. But there is, it seems to me, a problem with the very assumption that individuals' avowed beliefs and adherences to ideological systems are necessarily determinative of their entire worldviews: Beliefs and adherences are simply not *lived* this way by many people in today's society—if, in fact, they were ever so lived by a majority. This is so for a variety of reasons, perhaps the most important being that independence of judgment is widely regarded as more valuable and even more virtuous than submission to any human authority (even one that claims to be backed by God or by history), and that for many people, even if they do not articulate the matter this way, the true and the good cannot be reduced to any system of propositions, however complex. What is often of greater importance for them than any such system is their "feelings," and it is a mistake to regard what are called feelings in this context as if they were mere superficial, fleeting "impressions," unrelated to intellection.

These are the kinds of considerations that lie, for example, behind the well-documented phenomenon whereby a large majority of married American and Western European "Catholics," who regard themselves as such, continue to practice contraception even though the set of dogmas to which they are supposed to subscribe clearly indicates a prohibition of this practice, and even though many (but probably not all) of these individuals are aware of the prohibition. From the standpoint of the highly dogmatic Catholicism that I learned as a child and that the new catechism and other initiatives taken by John Paul II are intended to revive with some modern twists, all such people *must* at best be lying to themselves, wallowing in bad faith, if they are not simply *lying*. But as I have tried to show, it is only from the standpoint of this dogmatic conception of "faith," which is foreign to so many of today's "faithful," that this is so.

The same kinds of considerations are of use to me in attempting to explain the belief structures of many intellectuals and ordinary people alike in Eastern Europe, or for that matter in the West prior to 1989, who regarded themselves as Marxist-Leninists but never accepted the often highly dogmatic, clear formulas that appeared in the diamat textbooks and defined this system of supposed truths. In fact, even though, especially at certain times and for intellectuals in particular, the threat of the kind of sanction represented by the 1953 "trial" of D. Michaltschev in Bulgaria[6] (or of an even more dire fate) was a very serious constraint, nevertheless Marxism-Leninism was in principle incapable of reaching the level of internal sanction that the religious threat of everlasting damnation can achieve, or even of claiming the degree of infallibility that follows from accepting a religious leader's assertions of divine inspiration. Thus, even for that ever decreasing minority who, at the time of the system's collapse, still considered themselves committed Marxist-Leninists, the collapse was not quite so traumatic (at least not for everyone in this category) as an external observer, persuaded by Western anti-Communist depictions of faceless, utterly rigid "true believers" in the system, might have been led to expect. Nor, consequently, is it really accurate to say that the apparent rapid evolution of thinking evidenced in the subsequent statements and actions of all such individuals has constituted nothing but a massive, self-serving manifestation of "bad faith."

This line of reflection is, as I hope, useful for understanding the case of an East European intellectual who, let us say, published books of relatively high philosophical quality under the old regime but included in them statements about the wisdom of Marxism-Leninism that he would not think (for intellectual as well as political reasons) of making today. In part, of course, those statements were efforts at self-protection. The authorities were much less likely to question, or perhaps even to refuse to publish,[7] his work if some such statements were included. And let us assume that that work was of genuine value for the intellectual community of the country in question. But was that the sole justification for his having included such statements? Probably not, in the specific case of which I am thinking. (And there are undoubtedly many more such cases that are roughly similar.) He remains today very much of a *gauchiste*, with a strong interest in political theory, including a strong critical stance toward the system of capitalism at least in its dominant current form. Before the collapse of 1989 he had presumably harbored hopes, *malgré tout*, that the government in his country and in the rest of the bloc might still evolve eventually into something more compatible with that critical spirit, less authoritarian, and more positive with respect to the distribution and cultivation of resources. Granted, we can see in hindsight, and indeed it was rather clear even at the time, that the 1970s and 1980s as a whole were years during which, if anything, the gap between this hoped-for[8] ideal and the "really existing socialism" of his country widened, especially in the country in question, East Germany, which had had a quite robust and even globally competitive industrial base during its earlier years under Communist governments but then declined precipitously. But there was still no *decisive* reason for concluding that a future reversal of this decline, under continuing Marxist-Leninist auspices of some sort, was utterly impossible; and hope is an important psychological force, if nothing else.

I have deliberately used the expression "Marxism-Leninism" to name the officially endorsed ideology regnant in the regimes in question; this was in fact a commonplace label used by the regimes themselves, in part to distinguish that ideology from any number of actual or possible alternative versions of Marxism that opposed important elements of this official ideology. "Western Marxism," a blanket term itself embracing a wide range of perspectives, had as a unifying theme, in almost all of its variants, a critical stance toward Marxism-Leninism, and this could also be said of the positions of members of the *Praxis* group in Yugoslavia. Thus, an East European intellectual who endorsed a certain understanding of Marx's philosophy but regarded the "official" Marxist-Leninist[9] version of it as an aberration or even a caricature would have been able, at least on an intellectual plane, to accept the collapse of the old regimes with a considerable degree of equanimity (or even pleasure). This was, in fact, the reaction of more than a few "Western Marxists." The intellectual lives of such individuals, both Eastern and Western, then, may rightly be seen as characterized by more continuity than change over the 1989–1990 period, even if some other aspects of the Easterners' lives changed drastically.

We do need to confront cases of genuine conversions of individuals' worldviews, cases in which adherence to some version of Marxism-Leninism or of Marxism *tout pur* has been replaced by any one of a number of alternative ideological commitments apparently inimical to any Marxian orientation. On the surface or in aggregate, of course, such cases of true "conversion" appear to be the most numerous of all. I hope through my categorizations and reflections up to this point to have cast some doubt on this appearance, even though there are no reliable statistical surveys on the subject; but, even more, I hope to have shown some of the reasons *why* any such surveys that might be undertaken would be incapable of capturing the complex and subtle variants of human belief commitments with which we have to deal. Just as sheer opportunism, difficult (at least in the case of intellectuals) though perhaps not utterly impossible to find in its pure form, constituted the limiting case at one end of the spectrum, so total, instantaneous conversion would constitute the limiting case at the other end, if, similarly, it could ever be found in complete purity. It should be clear that I am extremely skeptical about such a possibility.

It may be appropriate to revert, once again, both to religious analogies, because it is in this domain that the language of "conversion" finds its most frequent usage in English, and to Sartre, who made a number of references to the idea of "radical conversion" in his earlier writings about ethics and politics.[10] One of the most famous religious conversions is that of Saul of Tarsus, who had persecuted Christians in support of the Jewish leadership and was said to have been blinded by a light, while traveling to Damascus to ferret out the Christians there, and told by a voice to persecute Jesus no longer. Other famous religious converts, whether from one religious sect to another (e.g., John Henry Newman, later a Roman Catholic cardinal in England) or from comparative irreligion or indifference to religion (e.g., St. Augustine) or from respectful atheism to a devout life (e.g., Edith Stein), were not given quite such instantaneous, dramatic assistance as was St. Paul, the erstwhile Saul (if we accept the account given in the Acts of the Apostles). For some, the process of conversion has consisted of a combination of some important episode (e.g., in Stein's case, a reading of the autobiography of Teresa of Avila) with a longer-term sequence of events.

It is interesting to note that all four of the converts whom I have mentioned had keen philosophical minds. Newman, in fact, even undertook a most interesting philosophical analysis of the very phenomenon under consideration here—the phenomenon of belief.[11] What seems to me to be a common characteristic of all of their histories, and so, I would infer, of countless comparable religious conversion stories, is that in hindsight the narratives of their lives, focusing on the radical personal or internal revolution that constituted their conversions, can at the same time be understood in very evolutionary ways, so that someone reflecting on them is easily led to say, "Yes, I see now why it was fated to turn out that way, why so much of what had preceded and seemed alien to his or her later life was in fact leading up to the conversion." (I am using the word "fated" here as a convenient colloquialism, without necessarily implying guidance by transcendent forces.) In other words, underlying continuities, sometimes very striking ones, are to be found both prior and subsequent to the conversion experiences.

Sartre attempted to deal with problems arising from his highly discontinuous conception of human consciousness as "being-for-itself" in his early philosophy by means of an interesting notion, not very fully worked out in the book *Being and Nothingness*, in which he introduced it, that he denominated the "fundamental project." Such a project, though always sustained by free choice and never amounting, for Sartre, to a karma, could be used to account for the fact that most humans' lives are in reality not constantly being recreated ex nihilo. Even in his last significant philosophical undertaking, *The Family Idiot*, Sartre used this tool to trace the development and come to a deeper understanding of the personality of Gustave Flaubert, the famous nineteenth-century French novelist. Perhaps the most successful of all instances of Sartre's use of this notion is his autobiographical effort at understanding himself by retracing his childhood and early adolescence, *Les Mots*. The *literary* project of self-immortalization that is captured in the title was indeed, according to his self-understanding, his own fundamental project and remained so even after, as he tells it in his rather dramatic concluding comments, his illusions about his own importance and about the importance of writing alike fell into smithereens and he underwent a "conversion" in which he was "led systematically to think against myself to the point of gauging the obviousness of an idea by the displeasure that it caused me."[12] Applying this notion of fundamental project to the life of Saul/Paul, I am inclined to give his project the label of religious zealotry. (I would certainly not apply the same label to religious converts across the board, however.) Paul's goal became, in fact, that of converting *others*; but he achieved success in pursuing that goal by appealing to *continuing* elements in would-be converts' lives, such as the "unknown god" whom the Athenians already worshiped as a part of their Pantheon, and in short by being "all things to all men."

Let us now reconsider the phenomenon of conversions away from Marxism-Leninism in the light of my religious conversion models. For many of those who can be said to have experienced a conversion, the process was in fact of several years' or even several decades' duration. One prolific and widely known philosopher who perhaps falls under this category is Polish thinker Leszek Kołakowski. His career includes a period of youthful party fervor in the 1950s, of serious (critical) scholarly work on medieval and contemporary Catholic thought, of fame as a dissident intellectual when a certain amount of dissidence was barely tolerated in Poland in the late 1960s, and then of teaching and writing in the West—primarily in England and the United States—in a spirit of increasing hostility, not merely toward Communist authorities and the totalitarian climate of thought that they cultivated but also toward Marxism as such. He gave frequent advice to the intellectual framers of Solidarnosc during its formative years. In 1986 he was selected Jefferson Lecturer,[13] a very prestigious honor, by the National Endowment for the Humanities; this is politically significant by virtue of the highly conservative ideological cast of the endowment's top-level leadership during the later Reagan years.

The high intellectual quality of at least some of Kołakowski's work is, to me, unquestionable. For example, the collection of essays from his "Marxist humanist" years, which is entitled, with suggestively confusing divergence, *Toward a Marxist Humanism* in the American version and *Marxism and Beyond* in its British counterpart,[14] contains some brilliant, perceptive, often witty analyses of the dilemmas of the East European intellectual of a generation ago; the German title of a similar collection, *Der Mensch ohne Alternative*,[15] has always seemed to me to epitomize perfectly the one-dimensional universe of thought with which so many in situations like his were confronted. (Whether it was Kołakowski who chose one or all of these titles is unknown to me, but for my purposes that does not matter.) Moreover, his three-volume study, *Main Currents of Marxism*,[16] is obviously a work of considerable erudition. It reflects his evolving disaffection with the entire Marxian and Marxist traditions from beginning, as it were, to end, a disaffection that has been reflected in many of his more recent writings.

To an outside observer like myself, Kołakowski certainly appears to have undergone a sustained process of ideological conversion. He came to find serious fault with some of the very ideas that had once seemed to underpin his philosophical work. A good example of this later fault-finding is his attack on the concept of "alienation" and related notions, to which I shall return in a moment. But he himself, I am confident, and indeed anyone undertaking a systematic analysis of his writings who wished to do so, would find numerous threads of continuity in his thinking from the start of his career, or at least from the time when he first began to question the pro-party attitudes of his earliest adult years, right up to the present—for example, his rejection of absolutism wherever it is found. Kołakowski could point out that he had tried to work within the existing system and situation in Poland when it had seemed plausible, however remotely so in retrospect, to think that the system might eventually evolve in a democratic direction on its own. He had loudly and publicly denounced it when, ten years later, it had become clear that that prospect was a hopeless one. And he could also point to the short, thesislike statement of seemingly disparate belief structures that he considers mutually compatible, "How to be a Conservative—Liberal—Socialist," which appears in a more recent collection of his essays.[17] Conversion? *What* conversion? Only a certain evolution.

Kołakowski's attack on *Entfremdung* (alienation) and, incidentally, on some related concepts ("*dialektisch, Struktur, Humanismus, Verdinglichung, Befreiung*") appeared in "Die Sogennante Entfremdung," an article published in 1978 in a journal of Austrian Social Democrats, *Zukunft*, as one side of a debate on the topic of the value of Marx for contemporary thought;[18] the more "positive" side of the debate was argued by Willy Brandt![19] It occasioned an unwontedly (at least for the time) heated attack by Yugoslav *Praxis* philosopher Mihailo Marković,[20] which, along with the original article by Kołakowski, I used as a starting point for my contribution to a Festschrift for Marković that was published in Serbo-Croatian in Belgrade in 1987. Entitled "Marković's Language and the Spirit of Community," it was a tribute to an old friend for whose philosophical stances I had great admiration.[21] Since the appearance of this volume, of course, former Yugoslavia has dissolved, and Marković became identified as a defender of the regime and policies of the profoundly nationalist president of Serbia, Slobodan Milošević, serving for a time as vice-chairperson of Milošević's Socialist Party. If the apparent intellectual, political, and personal tensions were not so evident (for example, I explicitly took Marković's "spirit of community," as discussed in my article, to embrace human community from small-scale to global, the latter through the implementation of ideas of federalism, and documented all of this in his writings), I would not feel inclined to interject my own involvement, which in a larger sense is quite peripheral, into this picture. Marković had been the incorruptible defender of a generous-spirited, forward-looking Marxist humanism, a person who showed unswerving solidarity with his colleagues when they were being persecuted by the Tito regime in the 1970s and he was offered the opportunity of special, more privileged treatment. His apparent conversion to spokesperson for Serbian nationalism in the midst of a brutal war that it had, willy-nilly, helped to spark has occasioned great dismay among many who have known him; and he has been very widely known.[22]

How, then, did Marković's astonishing "conversion" (if it indeed is one) come about? Once again, as in the case of his erstwhile intellectual antagonist Kołakowski, but perhaps in this case with even greater explicitness and sense of certainty, we encounter a denial that there has been a fundamental conversion at all. Times and circumstances have of course changed, over and over; as the war in Bosnia was winding down in late 1995, Marković was ousted from his party position and *eo ipso* placed once again, but now under drastically altered conditions, in the role of "dissident." But he has continued to see himself as a proponent of "democratic socialism," and Serbia and Montenegro (which constitute present-day "Yugoslavia") as the objects of vicious slanders and misrepresentations in the international press, in large part because they are the one part of Europe that tried to remain faithful to the democratic socialist ideal.[23] He is, as far as I can tell, completely sincere in his affirmations. But few of those among my own acquaintances who have been familiar with him and his ideas over the years fully accept his assertion of fundamental continuity.

Of course, the skein of events, on a number of levels, that has produced this appearance of a dramatic conversion on the part of a philosophically and politically prominent figure is in fact very complex. It seems to me true as a matter of principle that no one individual, including Mihailo Marković himself, can have a full grasp of all of them, but it would be possible for me to enumerate quite a few: for instance, facts concerning the evolution of the Yugoslav Federation in the years just before the war; historical events (which have been widely cited by, among others, Marković himself) going back to the Battle of Kosovo in 1389 and perhaps earlier; the economic recession in Yugoslavia and on a global scale in the late 1980s and early 1990s; changes in leadership in the Serbian Academy of Sciences during the same time period; personality factors; perhaps even physiological factors. But that would be the subject of a book in itself. What most concerns me here and throughout these reflections is the light that such cases as this one may shed on larger questions about human reality.

Although standard histories of the Western intellectual tradition do not insist a great deal on this fact, there are few thinkers, major or minor, of any significance in this tradition who cannot be said to have changed substantially in their outlooks over the course of their careers. In some cases, such as those of Hobbes or Kant, what they did early in their careers is (relatively) discounted by the historians because it was discounted by the thinkers themselves. Hobbes was launched into his later way of thinking when, in his fifties, he read Euclid for the first time, and Kant distanced himself from the "dogmatic slumbers" of his earlier years. In other cases, there may even be a preference on the part of some critics for the earlier works—Marx, Sartre, Husserl, and Heidegger[24] are four examples that come immediately to mind. Aristotle in his old age expressed a liking for the myths that seem almost totally excluded, at least as serious objects of study, from the uncompromisingly analytic writings that we know as his *corpus*. And Plato evolved in significant ways, not only with respect to the meaning of the theory of forms, but even with respect to such diverse questions as the degree of what we would call authoritarianism that he favored in the political sphere. (It is much greater in his late-life work, the *Laws*, than in the *Republic* or the *Statesman*.) In many instances, the differences are so great with respect to some important questions as to constitute a total repudiation by the later individual of what he (or, in too few cases in the histories, she) thought. And yet one can also, and always, discover great continuities, across the individual's life span, in areas of concern and in overall ways of approaching the world. Thus the phenomenon of intellectual "conversions" under the force of circumstances, which may at first have seemed startling, as in the recent history of Eastern Europe, is perhaps more of a rule or norm than an exception; only the brevity of the time period during which, in this case, we can observe sizable clusters of such apparent conversions may be slightly unusual.

One may further be justified in asking whether, in principle, this phenomenon is a good or a bad thing. My own inclination is to say that it is in principle good, on the ground that we should expect individuals' outlooks on reality to change over time in response to ongoing experience(s).[25] Lived experience is to me the origin of much of what is valuable in philosophy and in thought in general, and concerning those who have not changed it is reasonable to ask how much they have truly lived. So much for the matter of principle. On the other hand, by no means are all such changes necessarily positive; that is the chance that one takes. The elimination of some barriers to freedom of intellectual expression in Eastern Europe has led to great innovations and intellectual productivity in some cases; in others, to sterility or even to calls for the erection of new, though different, barriers. Facile generalization is impossible.

The most tempting reaction, it seems to me, to the history of apparent "conversions" that are contested as to their significance and reality even, and often especially, by those who have undergone them is one of total skepticism about beliefs and ideas in general—a universal throwing up of hands. There are countless stories of individuals who fought, and in many instances risked or even sacrificed their lives, for what they sincerely regarded as lofty and supremely worthy ideals under the banner of the hammer and sickle; it is reasonable to speculate that many of them, if they were still alive, would be joining in the chorus of condemnation of the historical Communist movement. We do indeed have cause to wonder, when we step back from our particular hobbyhorses of the moment, whether anything really *matters* in a permanent way. Someone could respond that all ideologies—philosophical, political, religious, and so on—may indeed be dubious and tainted in view of their ultimate instability and their capacity to turn out in practice to be the reverse of what their most ardent believers had taken them to be, but that there are still certain irreproachable abstract values that might ultimately be called "decency." To this, there is an obvious retort: The insistence on decency has often led, throughout human history, to practices of the most intolerant and oppressive sort.

But skepticism itself, as Hegel[26] among many others has well shown, is an unstable attitude, unlikely to endure very long. Even the partial skepticism of the postmodern attack on grand narratives, which has sought to undermine systematic thinking on a global scale while allowing limited, partial explanation to survive, has given way in the mid-1990s to renewed talk of eternal values[27] and/or sweeping condemnation of the hegemony of contemporary world capitalism in the name of Marx's ghost.[28] Simply retreating to individual self-cultivation, in line with the sentiment expressed by G. E. Moore in the final paragraph of *Principia Ethica* that "unmixed good may all be said to consist in the love of beautiful things or of good persons,"[29] although an attractive option in many ways, is practically impossible in human communities, which are interdependent on all levels and necessarily extend well beyond small circles of close friends. Thus, intellectual arguments about the proper way to live, involving as they must alternative visions of the past, present, and future of human society and therefore the possibilities of both radical change and continuity, will not and cannot be abandoned despite all the incentives to total disillusionment and "opting out." The best one can hope is that the conversation[30] will be carried out with intelligence and clarity, with mutual respect involving the avoidance of needless hurt or harm, and with a vivid awareness that perfection in this world is unachievable by individuals, institutions, or thought systems.

Notes

1. Although ours is a society in which pressures to "reveal all," all the time, are enormous, I intend to try to conceal certain names here because I regard privacy as a value that should still be respected *ceteris paribus*. Thus the vignette that I have just offered is accurate, to the best of my memory and knowledge, but I shall not name the individual in question. In some cases, however, preserving anonymity will be impossible, or undesirable as far as I am concerned, or both.

2. See, for example, Phyllis Morris, "Self-Deception: Sartre's Resolution of the Paradox," in *Jean-Paul Sartre: Contemporary Approaches to His Philosophy*, ed. H. J. Silverman and F. E. Elliston (Pittsburgh: Duquesne University Press, 1980), 30–49; Lewis Gordon, *Bad Faith and Anti-Black Racism* (Atlantic Highlands: Humanities Press, 1995); and Joseph Catalano, *Good Faith and Other Essays* (Lanham, Md.: Rowman & Littlefield, 1996).

3. Jean-Paul Sartre, *L'Être et le néant* (Paris: Gallimard, 1957), 109.

4. The notion of faith that was so central to the thought of Kierkegaard, which was itself so influential on Sartre at certain points in his intellectual development, seems to me to be different from this one in significant respects, but to discuss this matter here would take us too far afield.

5. Without wishing to insist on it and simply by way of establishing credentials, I was awarded a major Christian doctrine prize by the Roman Catholic archdiocese of New York when I was in eighth grade, which was at that time the standard final year of elementary school.

6. See W. McBride and I. Raynova, "Visions from the Ashes: Philosophical

Life in Bulgaria from 1945 to 1992," in *Philosophy and Political Change in Eastern Europe*, ed. Barry Smith (LaSalle, Illinois: Monist Library of Philosophy, 1993), 111.

7. It must be remembered that publishing, like most other significant industries in most of the countries in question, was a state monopoly under the old regime.

8. This aspect of the life of the spirit in the East Bloc was captured particularly poetically and at length, but more by anticipation than otherwise, by Ernst Bloch in *Das Prinzip Hoffnung* (Frankfurt-am-Main: Suhrkamp, 1959). Bloch himself eventually left East Germany to live in the West.

9. It should be noted, in passing, that none of this touches the question of whether or not official Marxism-Leninism was faithful to *Lenin*, even if it is granted for purposes of argument that it was not very faithful to Marx. But that is another story, which would take us too far afield for the moment. My own opinion of Lenin as a philosopher, which I have expressed in several places, is not very high. On the other hand, the intellectual awakening that we see him expressing in marginal notes during a reading of Hegel just prior to his death is, I think, not insignificant. In any event, Lenin was an intellectual giant by comparison with Stalin and his successors, and there is reason to wonder how Lenin might have reacted to some of the later dogma that was codified and diffused in his name.

10. See James F. Sheridan Jr., *Sartre: The Radical Conversion* (Athens: Ohio University Press, 1969). The theme is prominent in passages of Sartre's unfinished, posthumously published *Cahiers pour une morale*, although in some of these passages it takes on such an absolutist cast (the idea of a radical change in history) as to constitute, in my view, a *reductio* of the idea.

11. John Henry Newman, *An Essay in Aid of a Grammar of Assent* (New York: Longmans, Green, 1947).

12. Jean-Paul Sartre, *Les mots* (Paris: Gallimard, 1964), 210 (my translation). It is also important to note, in the present context, that Sartre saw himself as having undergone a more instantaneous type of conversion when, on vacation in Italy in 1952, he learned of the baseless arrest of French Communist Party leader Jacques Duclos and returned immediately to France to begin work on his long essay, "The Communists and Peace," which marks the beginning of the period of his closest alliance with the party (though he never actually joined it). See his account of this "conversion" in "Merleau-Ponty," *Situations*, vol. 4 (Paris: Gallimard, 1964), 248–49, and my discussion of it in *Sartre's Political Theory* (Bloomington: Indiana University Press, 1991), 93f.

13. The title of this lecture was "The Idolatry of Politics."

14. J. Z. Peel, translator. The U. S. publisher is Grove Press, 1968. The British edition (London: Pall Mall, 1969) contains the same essays, but with the addition of an introduction by Leopold Labedz that furnishes basic information about Kołakowski's early years and subsequent development up to the time of publication, including citations (pp. 6–7) demonstrating that he at first "conformed to Soviet shibboleths."

15. Leszek Kołakowski, *Der Mensch ohne Alternative: Von der Möglichkeit und Unmöglichkeit, Marxist zu sein* (Munich: Piper, 1967).

16. Łeszek Kołakowski, *Main Currents of Marxism*, P.S. Falla, tr. (Oxford: Oxford University Press, 1981).

17. Łeszek Kołakowski, *Modernity on Endless Trial* (Chicago: University of Chicago Press, 1990), 225–27.

18. Łeszek Kołakowski, "Die Sogennante Entfremdung," *Zukunft*, February 1978, 46–50.

19. Brandt was for a long time the leader of the German Social Democratic Party.

20. Mihailo Marković, "Leszek Kolakowski and so-called alienation," *Philosophy and Social Criticism* 5 (September–December 1978): 231–42.

21. "Markovićev Jezik i Duh Zajednice," trans. J. Kovačević, in *Filozofija i društvo*, ed. Dragoljub Mićunović (Beograd: Centar za filozofiju i društvenu teoriju, 1987), 33–44. One of three contributions by non-Yugoslavs, this article appears immediately after the initial long bibliography of Marković's writings. Retrospective ironies abound, for instance, the second contributor was Zagorka Golubović, a Belgrade philosopher who became a strong critic of Marković's subsequent political stances; and the editor, Dragoljub Mićunović, subsequently became the head of the Serbian opposition Democratic Party.

22. To cite just one recent bit of evidence in support of this, he was one of the contributors to a 1993 publication, one of a small number of such publications, of the International Federation of Philosophical Societies (better known by its French acronym, FISP) on *Philosophy and Cultural Development* (printed in Ankara, Turkey). His article, on pages 45–56, is entitled "Culture and the Prevalent Paradigm of Development."

23. Mihailo Marković, "Scholarship and ethnic cleansing," *Times Literary Supplement* 16 (July 1993): 15–16. The occasion was a Festschrift for the late C. B. Macpherson, *Democracy and Possessive Individualism: The Intellectual Legacy of C. B. Macpherson*, ed. Joseph H. Carens (Albany: SUNY Press, 1993), to which Marković had made a contribution. During the course of editing the book, Carens came under some pressure to exclude Marković's contribution because of the developments mentioned here. He decided instead to write a note preceding that essay in which he discusses the entire situation and is critical of one paragraph, added in early 1992, in which Marković defends Serbia and Montenegro and the old Federal Army of Yugoslavia. At the same time he solicited a very brief reply from Marković, which was printed, along with Carens's comments, in *TLS* in advance of the book's publication.

24. The case of Heidegger has additional interest by virtue of his well-known affiliation with Nazism, which may or may not be seen as a "conversion" but certainly must lurk in the background of the present discussion of former Communist intellectuals. I prefer not to complicate matters still further by introducing this case here.

25. I elaborate on this, apropos of Sartre and in general, in "Sartre's Concept of Freedom," *Phenomenological Inquiry* 16 (October 1992): 64–65.

26. Section B.4.B.2, "Skepticism," in *The Phenomenology of Mind*.

27. There is a hint of this in Jean-François Lyotard's more recent work, *Moralités Postmodernes* (Paris: Galilée, 1993), cited in a different context in chapter 2.

28. My reference here is to Jacques Derrida's *Spectres of Marx*, previously cited.

29. George Edward Moore, *Principia Ethica* (Cambridge: At the University Press, 1947), 224.

30. I am alluding to Richard Rorty's well-known revival of Michael Oakeshott's notion of philosophy as the "conversation of mankind." The Rorty of some fifteen years ago was widely and with good reason regarded as someone who considered most social and political philosophy to be misguided or worse. But more recently he has evolved to the following point, as encapsulated in a German newspaper account of a presentation of his at the 1993 World Congress of Philosophy in Moscow: "Rortys Appell an die soziale Rolle der Philosophen hielt es bewusst mit Marx: Die Philosophen hatten der Menschheit zu helfen, um die Zukunft lebbar zu machen." *Die Zeit* 39 (September 1993): 70.

Chapter Four

Theory and Practice: Philosophical Politicians and Philosophy as Political

Let us first recall Socrates' own fateful words:

> Cities will have no respite from evil, my dear Glaucon, nor will the human race, I think, unless philosophers rule as kings in the cities, or those whom we now call kings and rulers genuinely and adequately study philosophy, until, that is, political power and philosophy coalesce.[1]

We still laugh, as Socrates presumed that his interlocutors might, but our laughter is tinged with bitter historical experience. In this chapter I first examine a few of the reasons why Socrates' (Plato's) suggestion is necessarily misguided. Then I consider why, nevertheless, philosophy does potentially have much to contribute to politics and discuss some of the applications and misapplications of philosophical ideas to East European politics in recent times, highlighting the role played by the *economic* "philosophy" of privatization and the market.

An initial problem encountered when reflecting on the philosophy-politics admixture in light of the events in Eastern and Central Europe is a definitional one. It is relatively easy to define "politicians." They are the leaders either of governmental institutions or of opposition parties or groupings. But the class of "philosophers" is certainly not identical with the class of those who draw salaries from philosophy departments or institutes, any more than the class of "intellectuals" is identical with the class of college and university professors! In fact, there is probably a closer fit between the terms "philosopher," in the qualifiedly honorific sense in which I am intending it here, and "intellectual" than there is between "intellectual" and "college teacher." In my experience, at least, even philosophers of distinction who confine themselves to highly technical analyses tend to have a broad education and wide cultural interests.

In much of Eastern Europe, a tradition that antedates the bygone Communist era by decades assigns considerable prestige to the various institutes of its academies of science ("science" being taken in its broad sense to include philosophy) and assumes that there will be an incestuous relationship, or at least many commonalities and bridges, between these academies' leaderships and memberships, on the one hand, and government leaderships, on the other. This tradition has held (to varying degrees in different countries, as always) across the transitions to and from Communism. In the same tradition, political dissidents have often been persons qualified for potential academy memberships but barred from them by virtue of their dissidence. This serves as background to the current situation concerning intellectuals in politics.

Probably the best-known politician-intellectual is Václav Havel, a very distinguished author and former political prisoner. Havel is not a professional philosopher but a person with a considerable education in philosophy[2] who used to write about the incompatibility between the intellectual and political functions. He then rode a crest of popularity to the presidency of Czechoslovakia and then proceeded to oversee that country's division, which he opposed. Numerous other cases of political intellectuals in the recent history of Central and Eastern Europe can be cited: some of the creators and early mentors (including Leszek Kołakowski) of Solidarnosc, the movement and the party that eventually brought about the presidency of Lech Wałesa in Poland (eventually to be repudiated by him shortly before he lost reelection); conservative leader G. M. Tamás, a significant albeit quite eccentric force for several years in Hungary;[3] former President Želiu Želev of Bulgaria;[4] Mihailo Marković, whom I discussed in the previous chapter, as well as Dragoljub Mićunović,[5] Svetozar Stojanović,[6] and others in Serbia; even Gorbachev (at least through marriage, his once influential wife being the holder of an advanced degree in philosophy) in Russia; and so on. But the extent to which any or all of their "cities" have found a "respite from evil" (to revert to Plato's language) as a result of these apparent "coalescences" of philosophy with political power is at best limited.

If we assume that something went wrong, relative to the initial expectations, in some or all of these cases, what could it have been? The simplest answer, of course, is that well-intentioned philosopher-politicians were obstructed, in whole or in part, by less well-intentioned, or at least less insightful, domestic and/or foreign opponents. Like many "excuses," this one is partially true, but it is simply too superficial and self-serving to be taken seriously as an adequate explanation of failure in any particular instance. We need to reconsider the assumptions that have led to the high expectations that many people still have, despite centuries of skepticism about Plato's conception of philosopher-kings, concerning what philosophically minded individuals can accomplish in the political realm.

On what grounds are we supposed to accept the assertion, made in the text with which this chapter opened, that Plato ascribes to Socrates? Taken out of context, its promise of a less evil world *if* philosophy and political power should ever coalesce reads like sheer, unsupported dogma. Taken in context, its plausibility depends on an intricate, systematic Platonic account of the nature of all reality, involving the existence of an unchangeable realm of Forms, of which the Form of Justice in which republics ought to participate is one of the most important, and further assumptions concerning the possibility of knowing the structure of these Forms and the varying degrees of closeness or distance from them that participants are capable of exhibiting. Unless this entire, complex web of metaphysical claims (of which, of course, I have mentioned only a few elements) is accepted as true, we shall need to look elsewhere for support for the assertion attributed to Socrates about what philosopher-kings could do if given a chance.

The language of the citation gives Plato, if he were alive, and other defenders of this idea an easy way out when confronted with the observation that would-be philosopher-kings who *were* given some such chance, such as his friend Dion in Syracuse or Socrates' student Alcibiades in Athens or any of a number of our Central and East European contemporaries, had "screwed up" and failed, not only to achieve their political goals, but even to maintain respect for their own ethical-political principles. Ah, it could be said, but those individuals can be seen in retrospect not to have studied or practiced philosophy "genuinely and adequately," as the text puts it. But how, given the finitude of human life spans, can we ever be sure that *anyone*, Plato included, has ever studied or practiced philosophy "adequately"? We cannot; hence we can never have full confidence in the self-proclaimed wisdom of any would-be philosopher-king. Far more consistent than the believer in the inerrant powers of any proposed candidate for such a role is the Socrates of the *Apology*, who famously decided to accept the Delphic Oracle's pronouncement that he, Socrates, was the wisest of human beings when he came to realize that he was more lucid about the limitations of his wisdom than were any of the rival claimants to this accolade whom he encountered.

If, however, we favor this latter, Socratic conception of philosophy as *docta ignorantia* over the more Platonic conception of it as knowledge of the Forms, it becomes difficult or impossible, and at any rate rather disturbing, to imagine it "coalescing" with political power. For example, would we be more or less distressed at the thought of ignorant armies, representing rival governments, clashing by night if we were to be assured that these were *learnedly* ignorant governments of Socratic philosopher-kings? If philosophers duly impressed by the limits of their own and others' knowledge were to come to power, would they be less inclined to wield that power, especially military power, in the first place? Plato, for one, never seems to doubt the inevitability of warfare (even though he does at one point have Socrates make a plea for Greeks to avoid *civil* war). *Perhaps* philosophers convinced of their own and others' ignorance might be, on average, somewhat less inclined to wield the sword in haste. But even a simple, commonsense understanding of the ways in which political power situations in the real world often require immediate decisions to undertake forceful or even drastic actions leaves me with little optimism in this regard. In short, it is by no means obvious that an agnostic or skeptical conception of philosophy on the part of "philosopher-rulers" implies a much greater likelihood of the radical "respite from evil" that Socrates is alleged to have anticipated at such time as philosophy and political power might coalesce.

The alternative, gnostic conception of philosophy that was Plato's own, on the other hand, undoubtedly does conduce to what mid-twentieth century writers labeled "totalitarian" attitudes in those philosopher-politicians who may think of themselves as having attained such gnosis. In this respect, Karl Popper's *The Open Society and Its Enemies*[7] makes a valid point, despite its numerous unfair and inaccurate claims concerning both Plato's thought and that of some later philosophers, notably Marx. If, on this conception of philosophy as absolute science, people who had the necessary ability and good will to study it to its heights and depths then became rulers, they would in fact be able to bring about a coalescence of political power and philosophy, by definition. But even on the assumption that this is a defensible conception of philosophy, such a state of affairs would logically result in a respite from evils due to internal causes in their "cities" only if those individuals' comprehensions of all the data relevant to decision making were flawless and no unforeseen factors arose.

V. I. Lenin is one important figure who utterly rejected Plato's idealist philosophy of Forms in favor of a very naive, straightforward materialist realism. Yet he seems to me to have adopted the spirit of Plato's thought with respect to the possibility of (virtually) flawless comprehension of the political world and of the "respite from evil" that would supposedly ensue in the long run. Lenin's combination of epistemological dogmatism and utopian political aspirations, far more than the philosophy of Marx, provided the ideological justification for the "totalitarian" spirit of the anciens régimes in Central and Eastern Europe.

Lenin certainly had many intellectual and personal strengths, but epistemology was not, in my opinion, one of them. Nevertheless, his principal venture into the domain of theory of knowledge, *Materialism and Empirio-Criticism*, served as a key basis for Marxist-Leninist dialectical materialism.[8] It upholds an ultrarealist view of the nature of human knowledge, epitomized in what is usually translated as the "reflection theory" of cognition. Lenin maintained that what is true about the world can be known with complete objectivity by means of the senses and that the entire Kantian heritage, with its insistence on the role of human consciousness itself in defining what we know and how we know it, must be dismissed as obscurantist, reactionary idealism. This view is an invitation to dogmatism, and it can readily be taken to imply, as Lenin took it, that those who have the most correct knowledge should promulgate it and use it as the basis for a political praxis that is virtually guaranteed to be successful to the extent to which they can induce other individuals, through agitation and propaganda and, if need be, coercion,[9] to see things "correctly" as well. Lenin's view does not rule out the possibility of error; indeed, the history of the rise of the "Bolsheviks," the eventual majority in intra-party struggles, over the "Mensheviks" and other rival political groups prior to the Russian Revolution may be seen as having been, in Lenin's eyes, the slow and perilous rise to ascendancy of those armed with the truth over vast multitudes mired in error.[10]

When expressed as blatantly and simplistically as this, the position in question will no doubt appear to most of us as obviously, and one might also add inhumanly, wrong. But the logic of it, once one accepts the initial premise of the possibility of obtaining objectively correct knowledge concerning at least the political domain, seems impeccable. Moreover, it is more or less the same logic, though based in a quite different worldview and expressed with more reservations and in more honey-coated language, that guides many a supposedly "democratic" regime, including certainly that of the United States, as well. Lying behind and reinforcing the obvious contemporary hegemony of U. S. "culture"[11] worldwide, including large parts of Central and Eastern Europe, is, it seems to me, a somewhat vague but serious conviction that the "American way" is "right" or correct and even, in light of the collapse of the anciens régimes and the rise to ascendancy of truth over error that these developments supposedly represent, demonstrably so. This "rightness," it is widely believed (again, all of this is very vague by comparison with Lenin's views, but the beliefs are nevertheless very real and effective, contemporary versions of the nineteenth-century slogan of "Manifest Destiny") must be based in certain principles that constitute an American ideology; might "political liberalism" be a suitable name for it?[12] At any rate, a linkage between philosophy and politics within the American context is implied which, although it is by no means a mirror image of the philosophy-politics connection depicted in Marxist-Leninist literature in its heyday, invites interesting comparisons with the latter. True, there are few professional philosophers of whom I am aware occupying important political positions in the United States today, but this may simply be due to the intense, excessive professionalism of much of contemporary American philosophy and the demeaning inanity of American electoral campaign practices, so discouraging to talented persons with alternative career possibilities, together with the absence of a tradition of philosopher-intellectuals of the sort that I have identified in Central and Eastern Europe. That a close linkage ought to obtain between philosophy, understood in some sense, and politics (though not necessarily betweeen professional *philosophers* and politics) thus seems to be a fairly widespread conviction across different ideologies and worldviews, based as it so often is on the belief, whether reflectively (as in Lenin's case, pun intended) or unreflectively held, that there exist objective truths in the political domain.

It is not, to be sure, a universal conviction. Among those seen as constituting especially important moments in the history of Western philosophy, René Descartes is virtually unique in exhibiting practically no philosophical interest in the political sphere. This fact itself is very interesting, since Descartes has been so exceptionally influential. An inquiry into his reasons yields several diverse explanations, for instance, that he feared repression and persecution, the fate of many a dissident before and since, if he were to express himself on these matters in the highly divided and politicized world in which he lived; or that he was so "turned off" by the revolutionary ferment of his day as to be firmly convinced that viable existing institutions ought to be maintained at almost any cost; or even both of these at once.[13] Descartes' connections in fact included a political leader, Princess Elisabeth of Sweden, who was taken with his philosophy, corresponded with him regularly and invited him to spend time at her court (a successful invitation that indirectly led to his death, since the Swedish climate that winter proved too severe for his delicate health). When she solicited Descartes' opinions about some of the views of another quasi-philosopher/would-be politician, Niccolò Machiavelli, his answers were polite, brief, and somewhat evasive; he appears not really to have wished to join in the discussion. No doubt Machiavelli's unsavory public image had much to do with this reaction. But another explanation of Descartes' general attitude toward politics is to be found in the sharp distinction that he draws between the rational and historical orders, a distinction according to which it would be unreasonable to attempt to change the latter in the name of the former. The upshot is that, especially in his autobiographical *Discourse on Method*, he makes frequent, shoulder-shrugging allusions to the vast diversity of attitudes and customs in different cultures and adopts a dismissive attitude toward any thought of applying the rigorous, systematic approach of his new philosophical method to sociopolitical and cultural phenomena.

Such an attitude seems to me to be just as untenable as the opposite belief in the possibility of philosopher-kings, for reasons to which I believe that Descartes himself ought to have subscribed in his own terms. When he writes, as he does, as if the language of nations and/or nation-states ("Germany," "Mexico," "my country") were self-explanatory, he in fact violates his own spirit of universal doubt and treats contingent and temporally limited phenomena as if they were necessary and atemporal. By refusing to raise questions about the metaphysical status of any aspect of the social order, he imposes arbitrary limits on philosophy itself. In short, if I am correct, the allegedly hard-and-fast distinction between the rational and historical orders will not stand up to careful analysis. And in that case it would be absurd to deny the possibility that careful philosophical training and thinking may *in principle* be capable of making significant contributions to political life, regardless of one's views about the objective status of alleged "truths" in this domain.

What sorts of contributions, then, might such training make, minimally, to would-be philosopher-politicians, or to philosophers who counsel politicians? Above all, it seems to me, philosophy involves a sense of radical criticism. In addition, as a complement to this, it has a potential liberatory, utopian function, in the sense that radical criticism of existing states of affairs opens the way to alternative future possibilities. Both qualities are in very short supply in today's world, and there is hardly any region more in need of them than Central and Eastern Europe.

The official ideology of the Communist movement was rooted, historically, in the concept of *Kritik*, to recall the German word on which Karl Marx insisted as much as on any word in his vocabulary. As a philosophy student, he inherited it, of course, from Kant, whose great work was of relatively recent vintage at that time; it was very common coin among Marx's contemporaries. In his early writings, Marx brandished the idea of critique like a sword,[14] and he continued to invoke its spirit during the period of his mature work: the subtitle of his *Capital* is *A Critique of Political Economy*. Unfortunately, as everyone now agrees, the movement that arose out of this evident spirit of critique soon came to be dominated by dogmatists—one of history's innumerable ironies —, and so a great many East European intellectuals and ordinary people now feel a revulsion at anything connected with Marx's name. One important result of this is that it would usually be considered imprudent, to put it mildly, for anyone in a position to influence the course of policy in the countries in question to allude to Marxian theory in the course of examining the parlous condition of most of that region today. Yet Marx's philosophy, as I have repeatedly argued,[15] is an extremely rich lode—probably the richest our global culture currently possesses—from which to mine intellectual resources for such an examination.

As for the utopian function of philosophy, that is somewhat more controversial. Many philosophers are reluctant to engage in any speculation about the future, much less in attempts to predict it. Marx himself exemplifies this aversion in the style, language, and conceptual framework of *Capital*,[16] despite strong elements of utopianism in his early writings, numerous comments in his personal correspondence expressing enthusiasms (usually short-lived) about the course of the future based on current events, and some stirring rhetoric in the *Communist Manifesto*. To some, talk of visions of a possible future smacks of fiction writing or even poetry, which they insist on distinguishing sharply from philosophy. But such alleged sharp divisions are in the last analysis just conventional and stipulative, and the work of many prominent modern philosophers, such as Kant, Nietzsche, and Dewey, has been enhanced and completed by their imaginative references to diverse such visions, which are vastly different in style and kind from one another, to be sure. Western philosophy has always been thought to have as one of its principal missions the liberation of human beings' minds from the thrall of conventional opinions and by that very token a liberatory opening up to alternative beliefs and behaviors thenceforth. Thus some expectation of a future different from the past and the present is inherent in the very enterprise. "Utopian" thinking parts company with philosophy, I suggest, only if and when it strains credulity too much by envisaging futures that cannot be shown to have sufficient feasibility or at least plausibility.

With these considerations about the aims of philosophy as background, let us now reconsider what confronted Central and East European intellectuals—professional philosophers and others—around the time of the great events of 1989. It was a rather simple task to identify the worthiest object(s) of radical social criticism: the authoritarian, often highly corrupt, Communist regimes that had exerted a stranglehold over the region for so many years. The general character of the much brighter, better future that now appeared feasible was also easy enough to articulate. It would be democratic and nontotalitarian, without governments dominating every aspect of daily life—in short, an open society.

But the devil lurked in at least two places: in the details, as always, and in many aspects of those Western societies in which an unquestionably greater official commitment to certain personal freedoms made them appear, to not a few intellectuals "from the other side," as model open societies, that is, "really existing" utopias. First, it was a mistake—understandable in light of past frustrations and great sufferings, but a serious mistake nevertheless—to treat *everything* about the old regimes as inferior, as I have heard (or at least did hear a few years ago) more than one Eastern European and Russian philosopher do. Such an attitude was implausible on the face of it: it was a simplistic reverse totalitarianism of thought. The perceived, often quite real, danger incurred by those who cited Marx during the early years after 1989 was one obvious manifestation of this error. Second, it was a complementary, and perhaps even more fatal, mistake on the part of many (by no means all, probably only a vocal minority of philosophers) to give effusive praise to contemporary Western capitalist society as a model society. Initially, many important distinctions (e.g., between formal freedoms of speech and actual access to major media) were overlooked in the process of eulogizing the West, and criticisms of it that had been commonplaces under the earlier regimes were often automatically dismissed as invalid; many of them (concerning, for example, crime rates, unemployment, and homelessness) had in fact been accurate enough.

The erroneous attitudes that I have just described were more characteristic of certain younger and/or "middle-level" intellectuals than of most of those, such as the individuals whose names were mentioned earlier in this chapter, who came to play leading political roles in the post-Communist world. The latter group were on the whole aware of a certain "grayness" about the truth, especially with respect to Western societies; many had actually traveled to the West at one time or other. What *did* characterize many of them in the first few years, however, was a certain sense of optimism and a certain expectation of friendly assistance, especially economic aid (as distinguished from profit-generating loans) from these much wealthier countries. This was, for reasons that I shall be considering shortly, a misguided optimism, utopian in the pejorative sense,[17] that seems to me to have colored much of their efforts to put theory into practice in the name of a better future for their own nations. Moreover, just what was the theory or theories to be implemented? Once past the vague concepts, often little better than slogans, of "democracy" and "open society" that I have already noted, the philosopher-politicians diverged markedly and sharply from one another, with no common core of theory similar to that which had characterized "official Marxism-Leninism in its heyday, however distorted by a combination of stupidity, repressiveness, and sheer opportunism. The three Serbian philosophers mentioned earlier, together with some of their less internationally prominent but also politically involved colleagues, are a good small-scale example of my point here. While never in fact uniform in their thinking, they had exhibited considerable philosophical as well as personal solidarity when their *praxis* philosophy movement had come under sharp fire from the Tito regime in the 1970s. But as their country evolved and devolved in 1990 and 1991 they self-consciously took a number of different and mutually incompatible theoretical and political directions.

Amid all this disarray in post-Communist theory and practice throughout the region, however, one ideological position has tended to assert itself in a comparatively monolithic way, a position for which trans-national institutions already existed and appropriate practices could almost instantly be developed to aid in its implementation. This is the ideology of "privatization." A term of recent currency (it was first popularized by British prime minister Margaret Thatcher less than two decades ago), it soon rose, with the help of widespread media support and a coincidental loss of heart and commitment on the part of much of the Left, from the status of contested concept to that of unquestioned slogan, a status that it continues to have for many. Among the vast majority of economists, it would seem, the idea that private ownership is in every case preferable to collective ownership and even, in most cases, to public *control*, has acquired the status of a faith that requires no argument in its defense. At most, it is thought sufficient to point to the collapse of, precisely, the anciens régimes of Central and Eastern Europe, with their varied but generally high percentages of collective ownership of economic resources, to consider the point made conclusively. It is not a theory in any recognizable sense, but it functions similarly to a genuine theory in giving direction to political practice.

So *economist*-politicians have come to play the roles of philosopher-kings in a number of the countries in question here. Harvard economics instructor Jeffrey Sachs dictated policy changes to the Polish government, for example,[18] and also gave a great deal of advice to the Russian government at a certain time. The policy direction of the Czech Republic, especially since its split from Slovakia and the decline of Havel's influence, was strongly determined by its early president, Václav Klaus, an economist (one whose insistence on privatization and the market, however, was *somewhat* tempered, in contrast to many of his professional colleagues, by a repeatedly articulated concern for maintaining adequate social welfare protections). And, towering above all single individuals, as time passes, the International Monetary Fund has begun increasingly to insist on privatization policies as a precondition for granting development loans to countries throughout the world (not merely in this region of it), for which such loans are a sine qua non for participating in global trade and having any share at all in global economic activity.

The IMF and allied banking institutions control, directly or indirectly, enormous financial resources, the fruits of decades of capitalist accumulation in the world's wealthiest countries. It is no surprise that in relatively small and historically poor and less industrially advanced countries the governments are prepared, in order to secure the largest possible amount of funding under *comparatively* favorable terms, to acquiesce in those institutions' ideologically driven demands for privatization and other "reforms" to ensure the dominance of the market in virtually all aspects of social and political life. Such countries are likely to prosper more, or at least suffer less, than countries whose governments try to resist some of these demands and are consequently refused access to the same resources. No special intelligence, much less brilliant economic insight, is needed to infer this correlation, based as it is on simple coercion. The view of those controlling the resources is, of course, that the resources are *theirs* and that they (a large, complex "they," to be sure) therefore have every right both to profit from them and to dictate the terms of their use—impeccable capitalist logic. The result, as observers from diverse perspectives are now coming increasingly to see, is a highly authoritarian, if not quasi-totalitarian, global system in which this simplistic and single-valued logic (the value in question being economic profit) tends to determine, to an ever greater extent, all aspects of life, social and even private, particularly in the needier countries such as those of Eastern Europe.

Enormous contradictions, portending probable deep rifts in our "one world" of the future, characterize this current state of affairs. At the economic level, as statistical table after statistical table shows, the imbalance between rich and poor both within and between countries keeps growing in most instances; the United States itself is no exception in this regard. At the international level, the pretense of state sovereignty, which was never a *total* fiction even in those nations of Central and Eastern Europe that lived, before 1989, under the discipline and yoke of the Soviet-dominated Warsaw Pact, is becoming increasingly just that, mere fiction, for all but, *perhaps*, the economically and militarily most powerful countries (or single country, the United States). And at the sociocultural level, conceptions of a good or desirable society that are alternatives to the profit-oriented consumerist model apparently accepted by most economists become increasingly difficult to defend as valuable or sustainable even as utopian visions. In short, the vague but once appealing notion of an "open society," the ideal of anti-Platonic philosophers concerned with politics, is being trumped on a global scale by the simplistic ideology of an overwhelmingly powerful capitalist economic system with the resources to enforce its "theory" in practice.

One exceptional individual in whose personality and activities these contradictions are very interestingly focused is George Soros. An emigrant from Hungary, he studied some philosophy in England under the tutelage of Karl Popper (himself an older emigrant from Eastern Europe), for whom he always retained great admiration even as his career interests shifted to the economic domain. He has channeled a great deal of his huge earnings into a group of international foundations, among which the Open Society Foundation (named, of course, after Popper's book and ideal) is particularly prominent. In one day's speculations several years ago, he brought about a humiliating devaluation of the British pound and reaped a very large profit for himself. His foundations, on the other hand, have as their objective to encourage openness and democracy, particularly in those societies on which we are focusing here, the societies of Central and Eastern Europe. He has publicly voiced concerns about some of the negative impacts of unbridled privatization and related practices to which I have been alluding, even while personally epitomizing the economic system in which they are embedded. In pursuit of "democratic" politics he has, by most accounts, frequently directed his various foundation offices and other enterprises in a quite authoritarian manner and has sometimes used his money to give potentially decisive support to national political candidates and parties that he has favored—in Ukraine, for instance. At the cultural level he has used his resources to support alternative institutions of his own devising, such as the Central European University in Budapest and elsewhere, which operates outside the jurisdiction of, and in certain ways as a challenge to, the established higher education systems of the countries in which it is located.[19]

Do I mean to condemn Soros, the quintessential philosopher-economist-political agent of contemporary Central and Eastern Europe, outright and without qualification? By no means. To pass judgment on the activities of this fascinating and, for the time being, very influential individual would be beside the point for my purposes, and any serious effort to do this would require analysis of many biographical and historical details that are beyond the scope of this book. I in fact know many who have profited from his foundations' largesse and who, to my mind, have made positive contributions and will probably make many more to their beleaguered societies; but this, once again, is beside the present point. What is useful and important to note in his case is the extent to which a philosophically inspired set of sociopolitical activities can and inevitably does produce unforeseen consequences (e.g., unexpected oppositions, sponsored projects that veer sharply away from the values of the sponsor, etc.) and "counterfinalize" the original intentions of the agent.

Such is, in fact, the fate not just of practical policy initiatives such as Soros's, which are generated on the basis of some general, if rather vague, theoretical orientation, but also, in an even more dramatic way, of political philosophies themselves. The philosophy of Marx is the most obvious modern case in point, but its fate is by no means unique.[20] Thomas Hobbes, for example, seems truly to have thought that rulers should strive to implement his principles, perhaps even to the point of having them taught in the schools in place of the "subversive" doctrines taught there in the past. To the best of my knowledge, this hope of his was frustrated, but we can be virtually certain that the outcome of any such implementation would have been deeply subversive of Hobbes's own ideas. One could cite the various strange uses, so distant from their creators' intentions, to which the philosophies of Nietzsche, Mill, Aquinas, Locke, and many others have been put. One could make a very similar case, be it noted, concerning the theoretical work of Adam Smith!

One possible lesson to draw from all of this is (to return to Socrates' initial assertion) that "cities" will have no respite from evil no matter what. But this should not preclude attempts by philosophers at *alleviation*, through methods of social criticism, through efforts at utopia construction, and even, from time to time, through making forays into the world of politics in the admittedly faint hope that the myth of Sisyphus is just a myth, after all.

Notes

1. Plato, *Republic* 473c-d, trans. G. M. A. Grube (Indianapolis: Hackett, 1974), 133.

2. See, for example, the interesting use that is made of his ideas by Martin Matuštík, *Postnational Identity* (New York: Guilford, 1993), 187–258.

3. G. M. Tamás's numerous philosophical works include *Les Idoles de la Tribu: l'essence morale du sentiment national*, trans. G. Kassaï (Paris: Éditions Arcantère, 1991), an especially quirky (to my mind) defense of nationalism that I have found particularly interesting.

4. See the reference to Želev's early philosophical career in McBride and Raynova, "Visions from the Ashes: Philosophical Life in Bulgaria from 1945 to 1992," in *Philosophy and Political Change in Eastern Europe*, ed. Barry Smith (LaSalle, Ill.: Monist Library of Philosophy, 1993), 123–24.

5. Mićunović, as previously noted, founded the Democratic (opposition) Party in Serbia; he later became director of the Democratic Center in Belgrade.

Among his many philosophical publications is a study of Thomas Payne: *Tomas Pejn: Prava Čoveka* (Beograd: Filip Višnjić, 1987).

6. Stojanović became special advisor to Dobrica Ćosić when the latter served, briefly, as president of the reduced Yugoslavia before running afoul of Slobodan Milošević. Many articles and several books by Stojanović have been published in English, as is true of his former teacher, Marković, with whom he came significantly to disagree on a number of issues as the breakup of former Yugoslavia proceeded. See in particular Stojanović's recent *The Fall of Yugoslavia: Why Communism Failed* (Amherst, N.Y.: Prometheus, 1997).

7. Karl Popper, *The Open Society and Its Enemies*, 2 vols. (London: Routledge & Kegan Paul, 1962).

8. V. I. Lenin, *Materialism and Empirio-Criticism: Critical Comments on a Reactionary Philosophy* (New York: International Publishers, 1970).

9. On this question see my essay "Non-Coercive Society: Some Doubts, Leninist and Contemporary," in *Coercion* (NOMOS XV), ed. J. Roland Pennock and John. W. Chapman (New York: Lieber-Atherton, 1974), 178–97.

10. It may be useful here to remind English-speaking readers of the events that gave rise to the names. When Lenin finally succeeded, through cajoling and manipulating delegates to a small conference of Russian opposition leaders in exile (held more than a decade before the revolution) in getting a bare majority vote endorsing his Jacobin preference for committed revolutionaries over mere sympathizers in the definition of who should count as party members, he seized the opportunity to proclaim his faction the "majority" (*Bolsheviki*) and the other one the minority; this was the origin of the name "Bolsheviks."

11. See my paper "Coca-Cola Culture and Other Cultures: Against Hegemony," in *In Labyrinth of Culture*, ed. Liubava Moreva (Saint Petersburg, Russia: Centre "Eidos," 1997), pp. 154–68; a revised edition is to appear in *Relativism: Science, Religion, and Philosophy*, ed. Chandana Chakrabarti (Lanham, Md.: Rowman & Littlefield).

12. This is, of course, the title of John Rawls's later collection of essays, which involve a retreat from some of the more sweeping claims made in *A Theory of Justice*, to a position of recognizing cultural limitations in his position. See Rawls, *Political Liberalism* (New York: Columbia University Press, 1993).

A very striking expression of some of the same attitudes that I have been delineating here, more forthright than in any of his previous writings, is to be found in Richard Rorty, *Achieving Our Country: Leftist Thought in Twentieth-Century America* (Cambridge: Harvard University Press, 1998).

13. See my article "Ontological 'Proofs' in Descartes and Sartre: God, the 'I', and the Group," *American Catholic Philosophical Quarterly* 70, no. 4 (1997): 556.

14. In his September 1843 letter to Arnold Ruge apropos of their plans for the *Deutsch-Französische Jahrbücher*, for example, Marx emphasized the need for a *"ruthless criticism of everything existing."* See *The Marx-Engels Reader*, ed. Robert C. Tucker, 2d ed. (New York: W.W. Norton, 1978), 13. Even though later in his career Marx regarded himself as having abandoned "philosophy,"

at least as it had been understood by the student and professorial circles of his youth, it seems simply indefensible to me to maintain that he ever ceased to be a philosopher in a broader sense, *especially* given his lifelong commitment to *Kritik*.

15. See William L. McBride, "The Pathos of European Political Philosophy after Marxism," *Journal of Philosophical Research* 19 (1994): 331–43, and "The Philosophy of Marx in the Wake of 1989: A New Appraisal," in *Reading and Renewing the Social Order*, ed. Yeager Hudson and Creighton Peden (Lewiston, N. Y.: Edwin Mellen, 1996), 343–65.

16. See William L. McBride, *The Philosophy of Marx* (London: Hutchinson; New York: St. Martins, 1977), chap. 6.

17. I would like to insist on the importance of retaining a utopian element in social and political philosophy, so that the pejorative sense of this word should not be considered the only or even the most important one, *pace* Engels's infamous attack on the various versions of what he termed "utopian socialism."

18. See Sachs's very interesting lecture account of his activities in Poland, *The Economic Transformation of Eastern Europe: The Case of Poland* (Memphis, Tenn.: P.K. Seidman Foundation, 1991).

19. As of this writing, for example, degrees at the CEU in Budapest are still granted through a higher educational institution in New York State.

20. See my article "The Practical Relevance of Practical Philosophy: Philosophers' Impact on History," in *Philosophy in Context* 13 (1983): 31–44. This has been reprinted in *Perspectives on Ideas and Reality*, ed. J. C. Nyíri (Budapest: Filozófiai Posztgraduális és Információs Központ, 1990), 66–84.

Chapter Five

Values

A few years ago the American philosophical scene was enlivened by the publication of Alasdair MacIntyre's broadside tome, *After Virtue*.[1] It claimed, among other things, that philosophical discourse from roughly the time of David Hume had gradually displaced the traditional ethical language concerning "virtue" with talk of "values," which are alleged to be of a logically different type from "facts." This malign development had by now suffused the social sciences and other areas of Western culture far beyond the circle of philosophers. "Virtues" (though not always the same ones, to be sure) had been the key concept, according to MacIntyre, in the ethical thinking of Aristotle, Augustine, Aquinas, and many other philosophers, in literary writings such as Jane Austen's, and in the self-images of numerous actual societies, from the Homeric Greek and the ancient Icelandic to the Golden Age Athenian and the medieval Christian. Among the villains, after Hume, in MacIntyre's creative reinterpretation of Western thought, Nietzsche and Sartre stand out in particular—the former for his call for a radical transvaluation of values, "shattering the old tablets," and the latter for his comparable insistence that values, though conventionally presented as givens, are in fact free human creations.

Pace MacIntyre, I intend here to write above all about "values" because that seems to me a more useful way of approaching important aspects of the changes in the contemporary societies of Eastern Europe, where virtues, especially if understood in MacIntyre's communitarian sense, and positive values are (as I shall show) in very short supply. I am much more sympathetic than he to the aforementioned ideas of Nietzsche and Sartre. I discuss freedom as a real but Janus-faced value; the failure of defenders of so-called traditional values to make much headway; the rise of revenge as an "antivalue" and the related issues of memory and of dealing with past mis/deeds; the enormous deficit, as I see it, in the value of justice, viewed from both domestic and global perspectives; and some of the ways in which the values thought to adhere to democracy and civil society have been undermined. Towering malignly above all other values in the current conjuncture, as I describe it, is the single value that I am calling "efficiency-for-profit."

"Transvaluation of values" (the expression of which the Greek equivalent was first employed systematically by Thucydides to describe what occurred in Athenian society during the crisis of the Peloponnesian War with Sparta) seems at first blush to capture quite well the swift evolution of moral thinking in Eastern European societies following the dissolution of the old regimes. What actually transpired was much more complex than that phrase would imply, but it has its uses in this context. A strong spirit of *community* antedated the Communist era and was often useful in promoting the "official" morality of that era, in which cooperation was emphasized over individual self-promotion. The Marxist-Leninist perspective on ethics was itself fundamentally riven with contradiction. First, there was the conviction, expressed in *The German Ideology*[2] and in other more or less canonical texts, that morality was a part of any given society's ideological "superstructure" and hence relative to different modes of production; then there was the spirit of an ethic of expediency for the sake of the party's aims that was expressed in the title and content of Trotsky's essay, *Their Morals and Ours*,[3] an attitude that was far from being repudiated even though the essay's author was; then there was a very deeply embedded moralism, rigorous and in many regards puritanical, expressed through the educational systems, the laws, and the media, and often proclaimed as being in sharp contrast with the "decadence" of Western societies; and finally there was a pervasive sense of cynicism, particularly in the later years of the regimes, that in effect encouraged ridicule with respect to this moralism, as well as sanctioning corrupt practices on the parts of many who were in a position to engage in them.

It is very possible, however, to live with contradictions, depending on just which ones; doing so is perhaps inevitable in complex modern societies.[4] When the political circumstances that had sustained East European lived contradictions in the area of morality changed rapidly and radically in 1989–1990, these contradictions gave way to others, not easy for anyone to sort out with complete clarity. It is to be expected, if my analysis of "conversions" in chapter 3 was basically sound, that not everyone's values would immediately and radically have been transvalued; far from it. But at the very least serious shifts—complex and often divergent—in prevailing views of what is most important, or most worthwhile, have surely taken place.

In most countries, to begin with, there is much greater freedom of public expression and less concern, particularly among writers and other public intellectuals, about running serious personal risks by being critical of the existing regime. (Croatia has been and may still be a salient exception to this,[5] and there are no doubt others, the seriousness of the risks being of course quite variable.) This is one effect of the changes of 1989–1990 that is widely perceived as unmitigatedly positive. If such freedom is seen only as a means to some further goals, then doubts may be expressed, given adverse socioeconomic conditions in many countries, as to just how valuable it really is; but a great many persons seem to share my conviction that it is intrinsically valuable.

At the same time, there has been, quite naturally in a postcommunist environment, a greatly increased emphasis on skill in finance and large-scale commercial transactions. "The West" (especially the United States and Germany) is considered the model for the successful pursuit of these values, and rightly so. But if, as is well-known, business enterprise in the "model" countries is not always conducted according to Marquis of Queensberry rules (a boxing reference that strikes me as a still very apt analogy despite the relative decline in importance of boxing among major competitive sports), how much more severe have been the abuses of the new economic system in countries in which the rules themselves were virtually unknown until a few years ago! In at least some of these countries, beginning with Russia itself, the ubiquity of fraud and massive unfairness in the process of turning state enterprises over to private ownership is seriously denied by no one. The collapse of the government-sponsored "pyramid" scheme in Albania, in which a very large percentage of the national population had some family member involved, is one of a chain of scandals in which the new entrepreneurship has gone awry and ruined many lives. Defenders of the capitalist ideal, however, point out that a system's value cannot rightly be measured on the basis of notorious abuses of it. And capitalist business practices continue to intrigue and attract many; the significant growth of business schools and courses is often cited as one obvious index of this.

In point of fact, the motivation to young persons who are talented and ambitious to try to become involved in entrepreneurship is such as to virtually compel many to move in this direction, whether they find it particularly attractive or not. For example, essentially noncommercial callings, such as the arts, liberal education, and sports, which often commanded comparatively attractive salaries and other perquisites under the former regimes, now tend, under the new commercialism, to be either hopelessly undercompensated or else permitted to survive only through heavy commercialization, such as the relentless, often degrading advertising of athletic products by their users. The deep irony, then, is that the freedom to choose one's life project is being severely restricted by the configurations of the new profit system (the supposed freedom to "choose" to engage in a career that will bring little or no compensation is no freedom at all), even while the enhanced freedoms of public speech and protest mentioned above have begun to be enjoyed.

Cheerleaders for the new values, who are numerous and very well compensated, respond that the "price" that the societies of Central and Eastern Europe are paying for the introduction of capitalism is small compared with the ultimate benefits, although there may be some slight "trade-off" of freedoms involved here with respect to a few relatively marginal activities. In any case, they say, freedom of self-expression and capitalist entrepreneurship "come as a package" and are inseparable. This typical line of thinking, like the commodity-fetishistic language in which it is so often expressed, strikes me as extremely dubious. To begin with, any such defense of the new values greatly underestimates the extent to which the forcible introduction of the postmodern capitalist system and the cultural "values" accompanying it has indeed involved coercion on a massive scale. Consider the language of the "economist-kings" (see chap. 4): The "discipline of the market" (a favorite expression) is to be imposed, workers are to be kept in line, governments are to be treated in carrot-and-stick fashion, and layoffs are to be pursued however great the pain because this is what is "required" (whatever that is supposed to mean). Of course those who speak and write this way contend, unrepentant paternalists that they are, that all of these prescriptions are acceptable because they are purely aimed at the ultimate, long-term good of the peoples on whom they are being forced. But even if this were unquestionably true, which it surely is not, one would hope for a little more logical consistency on the part of these individuals, who unceasingly insist, regardless of all evidence to the contrary, that theirs is the path of "freedom."

Moreover, it is not just the parlous condition of institutions of culture, the arts, liberal education, and so on, deprived as they have been of resources and forced for survival to make themselves less accessible (through higher fees, etc.) to the larger public, that constitutes the negative side of the "trade-off." In any case, the loss or serious deterioration of such things will not seem especially deplorable to many of the new entrepreneurs or their ideologues. A broader decline in quality of life has been allowed, and even encouraged, to take place in public goods virtually across the board—health services, transportation, heating, communications, personal security—for the majority who cannot afford to pay a great deal more for them than was needed before. This broad reduction in daily material well-being for all but the conspicuous nouveaux riches minority in much of Central and Eastern Europe, to which

I alluded already in chapter 2, must be considered when "trade-offs" are being calculated, if, for temporary purposes of argument, utilitarian calculation is to be the dominant mode of discussion.

The fundamental shibboleth of the defenders of the new values is that "freedom" of self-expression and capitalist entrepreneurship "come as a package," that is, are inseparable. Repeated as it is ad nauseam by high government officials, media reporters, and of course apologists for capitalist enterprises, this claim has come to epitomize the contemporary Western equivalent of what the same Western propagandists used to characterize as "the technique of the 'Big Lie'" in Communist Party pronouncements. Of course it is true that the entrepreneur, *qua* entrepreneur and as long as he or she continues to be what the ideologues unblushingly call a "winner" rather than a "loser" in the capitalist socioeconomic "game," has enormous freedom—the more so as governments are persuaded or forced to accept the notion that any constraints on entrepreneurial practices other than straightforward fraud are unfair and inimical to the society's "freedom" as such; but this claim amounts to little more than a tautology. On the other hand, neither the ordinary worker in most capitalist enterprises nor the unemployed person victimized by profit-driven "downsizing" nor the families of such individuals—in short, most of the members of the society in question—enjoy any comparable freedom by virtue of their roles in the economic system.

Capitalist enterprises are for the most part highly undemocratic institutions, particularly with regard to the relationships obtaining between employers and employees. This is such a truism, so indisputable as an empirical generalization, that the felt need to restate it here causes me embarrassment—less for myself than for the world order in which I live, where this point is regularly overlooked and fatuous pronouncements treating "capitalism and freedom,"[6] or capitalism and democracy, as mutually reinforcing concepts are so widely respected. (I return to the issue of *political* democracy later in this chapter.) In many capitalist places of employment, a certain free space is nevertheless allowed to workers, for a variety of factors—for example, antidiscrimination laws enforced by governments, psychological recognition that productivity in certain types of jobs diminishes when excessive discipline is enforced on the workers, and retention of some sedimented attitudes of humaneness or mutual respect even within the workplace—that are not necessitated by the internal logic of the capitalist system itself and that in some cases, such as antidiscrimination laws, are widely viewed as being inimical to the best interests of what capitalist apologists tend simply to call "business" as such, meaning the capitalist *model* of business. Within this arena, of course, the ultimate sanction is that of firing the employee, and the typical capitalist enterprise offers few if any mechanisms, under most circumstances, for remonstrance on his or her part when this occurs.

Truisms, truisms, the proponent of capitalist values may at this point agree. But that, they say, is just part of the efficiency of the system, as contrasted with the very well-known inefficiency of socialist enterprises, for example, under the old regimes of Central and Eastern Europe. There, it is said, it was often virtually impossible to fire even the most time-serving workers, and that is part of what was evil about the old system. One important question that this line of thinking raises, as I am by no means the first to note, is that of efficiency's place among values. Almost everyone agrees that it must not and cannot be regarded as the *highest* of values, since it is always necessary to ask for what purpose the particular efficiency in question is being advocated. It remains true, however, that with the advent of capitalist enterprise in the countries in question efficiency has come to be viewed as relatively far more important, as a value, than it once was. It is coming to be taken somewhat for granted that getting rid of an inefficient worker in the name of improving "the bottom line," the profit of enterprise that is capitalism's answer to the question of "efficiency for what?" is justifiable regardless, at least for the most part, by just how severe the worker's needs or those of his or her family may be.

Against this widespread tendency to elevate efficiency-for-profit to a place of near supremacy in an imagined value hierarchy, defenders of traditional values have offered little serious opposition and have rather, more often than not, adopted a stance of complicitousness. Among such defenders it seems suitable to consider first and foremost the Catholic Church, with its still great prestige and enormous membership. During the period of dramatic changes in Central and Eastern Europe it has been led by a man from that region. Pope John Paul II has allowed himself to be given considerable credit for the events themselves (how much truth there may be to this belongs to a domain of historical hermeneutics into which I have no wish to enter here), as was made clear during his triumphal visits to his native Poland, the Czech Republic, and other countries of the region. In principle, the Catholic theological-philosophical doctrine, articulated variously but with a *certain* amount of coherence and consistency (though much less than its most militant proponents claim) over many centuries, is antipathetic to the capitalist valorization of efficiency and profit over the needs of living human beings to which I have just been pointing.[7] In principle too there is a great deal in common between the Catholic Church's rejection of this capitalist value axiology and all those core aspects of Marxism that are epitomized in Marx's attack, in *Capital*, on "the fetishism of commodities"; it is this commonality that underlay, and underlies to the extent to which it still exists, the so-called Marxist-Christian dialogue that once had some hearing in Czechoslovakia and other parts of Eastern Europe,[8] as well as the "liberation theology" movement in Latin America. In his pronouncements and other actions, Pope John Paul II, acting clearly not just on his own but with the support of the so-called Roman Curia (which is the effective power behind the Papal throne), has paid lip service to the idea that capitalist ideology in its most rigid form does indeed endorse values incompatible with those of his church. Yet he has been dismissive of all aspects of Marxist thought, condemnatory of liberation theology and punitive to some of its leading proponents within the church, and at least for a time, until he began to become more disillusioned with the way in which Eastern Europe is evolving, increasingly accepting of capitalist principles.[9] Despite his extensive training and interest in philosophy[10] and his potentially useful experience in negotiating with Communist authorities during his tenure as archbishop of Krakow, he has spent, or (to express it in harsh language that nevertheless strikes me as more appropriate) frittered away, a large part of his moral resources in struggles against abortion rights, contraception (of all things!), and the equality of women within his priesthood. Some of the church's membership (it is very hard to say just how many) have actively supported him in one or more of these initiatives (the divisive and ongoing conflict over abortion rights in Poland itself is a good illustration); but the current negative birth rates in a number of Eastern European countries are surely easier to explain on the hypothesis that his dicta concerning sexuality and reproduction are being widely disregarded (combined with the obvious fact of economic anxiety and fears about the future of potential new children) than by supposing that there has been a general diminution of sexual activity in favor of abstinence, much less a great rise in the popularity of convent or monastic life!

In fact it is widely alleged, by defenders of "traditional values," that a heightened preoccupation with sexuality is a salient feature of the current values transformation in Eastern Europe, a feature that is shared with much of the rest of the world. I am simply not sure to what extent this is true, or even just what it means to say it. For one thing, it is precisely the Catholic Church's excessive preoccupation with sexuality in a censorious way that, as I have been suggesting, has abetted its posture of complicity with the rise of the capitalist social (or more accurately antisocial) values under discussion here. It is indeed the case that erotic and/or pornographic magazines now enjoy brisk sales at kiosks where they were banned before 1989; even in times of economic hardship for so many, pornography sells, in a typically capitalist way. But a fascination with the attractions of sex is of course not a novelty in this or any other part of the world, and the sexual repressiveness and puritanism of the old regimes in Central and Eastern Europe, although real enough, do not strike me as having been in any way comparable in severity to those of which one hears under certain revolutionary Islamic regimes, for example. In fact, abortions were generally permitted and even, depending on the circumstances, encouraged in the countries in question, with the salient exception of Romania, where, as one professor from that country candidly explained it to me many years ago, official policy in this area was based above all on the felt need not to allow the Gypsy population, with its traditionally high birth rates, to overtake the ethnic Romanian population. Permissiveness in abortion policy, it seems clear to me, is incompatible with *extreme* sexual repression, and one may therefore express doubt about the extent to which the events of 1989 brought about quite as total a change in values orientation toward sexuality as some have claimed. True, prostitution now flourishes openly in many places where it did not before,[11] abetted by economic conditions that make it an easier way of earning a living, for women willing to take this drastic course of action, than are many others. I feel quite uneasy, as an outsider to the societies in question, about drawing many comparisons between the past and the present in this regard, but in any case I am convinced that those self-styled "traditionalists" who at the same time align themselves with the standard contemporary capitalist mentality according to which sex can and should be utilized to enhance "the bottom line" have left themselves with little or no standing to deplore the new sexual ways.

Working much more effectively than values traditionalists to subvert the extreme emphasis on efficiency-for-profit that is the hallmark of the capitalist value system are the proponents of another deeply rooted value (or one should rather say anti-value) that has recently flourished widely in most of the countries in question, namely, revenge. The desire on the part of newly dominant right-wing and liberal (in the European sense of procapitalist) parties to extirpate all traces of the old regimes and the privileges that the *nomenklatura* held under them has led to measures aimed at removing from positions of authority, and sometimes also from positions without much authority, those who had held them under those regimes, regardless of what their precise roles and specific actions had been. This has been a particularly widespread (and particularly easy, given the locus of power of the new all-German state) practice in former East Germany, the well-known former espionage director of which, Markus Wolf, and some others have actually been put on trial for having effectively carried out directives of the old regime. "Restructuring" and phasing out of academic and other institutions has resulted in widespread dismissals and in the "colonizing," or taking over, of many positions by persons imported from the West. The East German case is a special one in several ways, including the fact that that regime was exceptionally repressive in terms of the very size of its network of government informants and in some other respects. But so-called lustration policies in former Czechoslovakia and laws to similar effect in Bulgaria and elsewhere have had, arguably, more drastic consequences for those societies as a whole than have the measures taken in Germany, since former East German citizens are just a minority in the new Germany (and, it should be noted, can be and frequently are treated as members of a "minority" in the pejorative sense of such treatment). My critical point, which has been made by many observers, is that *some* of those "lustrated" ("cleansed" from their positions) were in fact the best trained and most competent individuals in their institutions and enterprises. Subjecting all of them to a blanket expulsion, regardless of individual differences in their past activities has had the effect of subordinating desirable and needed efficiency to the spirit of revenge, of Nietzsche's *ressentiment*.

Of course, my assault on the glorification of efficiency-for-profit cuts two ways. If such efficiency is or should be regarded as of lesser importance than some other values, then the mere fact that depriving some former party members and affiliates of their offices or even of employment might result in lowered efficiency is not a serious argument against doing it if one is convinced that the complicity evidenced by their past membership was a sufficiently great evil, perhaps so great as to exclude even the possibility of forgiveness. I have listened to discussions in which such convictions have been expressed, discussions that have inevitably raised broader issues concerning legal and moral guilt, historical memory, and the role of forgiveness in public life.[12] The minimum that should be said, I believe, in opposition to these draconian and impractical convictions within the context of Eastern Europe is that many talented persons under the anciens régimes had no realistic alternative to participating to some degree in party or quasi-party organizations, unless they were to have decided to simply squander their talents. And many participated in a spirit of strong skepticism about the regimes, sometimes combined with a hope of contributing, at least in a small way, to their amelioration. For such individuals, the notion of moral guilt is of doubtful applicability, whereas that of legal guilt does not arise at all unless ex post facto laws aimed at convicting them retrospectively were to be passed—a practice that would carry the most serious risks for any notion of social trust. There is no acceptable alternative to dealing with questions of culpability on a case-by-case basis.

The related issues of whether to make public old secret police files and/or to convoke "truth commissions" to rehearse major events of the past are complicated; a detailed examination of various proposals would be required. In general, however, it seems preferable for many reasons, not the least of these being the likelihood of there having been considerable prevarication by the compilers, to restrict access to files, in most cases, to the specific individuals named in each of them. (This has been the most common practice, a practice for which the procedures mandated by the Freedom of Information Act in the United States—where, it should not be forgotten, government agencies such as the FBI have *also* been known to engage in political persecution!—serve as a partial, imperfect model.) As for whether it is better officially to rekindle bitter memories through government-sponsored "truth commissions" or to leave the performance or nonperformance of that task (together with the weighing of the question as to whether *all* of the memories are in fact bitter!) to journalists, historians, and philosophers, the former course seems virtually designed to encourage what I have called the antivalue of revenge and therefore to be undesirable as a general policy, although it would be quite unjust to block legal efforts by individuals to obtain redress for specific crimes committed against them under the former regimes. The latter course, though "messier" and very unpredictable in terms of its effects, is more appropriate for truly "open societies."[13] In the comparatively closed society of post-World War II Yugoslavia, an opposite policy of encouraging the suppression of memories was pursued. The Tito regime decided to omit from official school textbooks, and so on, mention of terrible deeds done by members of one or another of its nationalities against members of other nationalities during the war. It is still debated whether this decision had a more positive or negative effect in the short run. What is certain is that the process of what I have called "rekindling memories" that took place throughout that land, in the newly liberated media and in private conversations, around 1990 played a major role in the ensuing disasters. As we can see from this example, the matters with which we are dealing here are fraught with fragility. Exactly which precise policy to adopt is not, in my view, clear-cut *except* for the proponents of uncompromising unforgiveness and revenge.[14]

On the other hand, in this vast circus in which practical contradictions flourish unrestrained, perhaps more frequent than punishments of those once affiliated with the party have been cases in which former members of the *nomenklatura*, especially those in the sphere of (Communist) business as distinct from intellectual and political life, for example, have managed to maneuver themselves into roles as major owners of newly privatized firms, firms that in many cases they once managed. Then, often enough, they have gone on to take advantage of new laws allowing them to liquidate the firms' assets for their private profit—to the detriment, of course, of the firms' workers and even, depending on the particular case, of overall economic productivity. (This has been a particularly commonplace occurrence in Russia, although the call for taking official revenge against former members of the *nomenklatura* is no doubt weaker there than in many of the countries further to the west.) In such cases, of course, *personal* profit is the only "value" to be realized, whereas the only apparent victims of revenge are the newly unemployed workers and the societies at large rather than their former bosses.

It is little wonder, then, that genuinely alternative ideals, alternative sets of values, are in rather short supply in the Eastern Europe of today. Consider *justice*, for example, which was such a "hot topic" among philosophers and social theorists from various other disciplines a decade or so ago in the wake of John Rawls's success with his book *A Theory of Justice*, premised as it is on the rather plausible assertion that justice "is the first virtue of social institutions."[15] Rawls already had his devotees (among those who could read English) in the former Soviet Bloc countries by the time of the changes in 1989, and his book is translated into a number of Eastern European languages. But there is a serious flaw in his entire approach, one that is highly relevant to the situation that we are considering, which is expressed in remarks such as the following: "I shall be satisfied if it is possible to formulate a reasonable conception of justice for the basic structure of society conceived for the time being as a closed society isolated from other societies."[16] The idea that a useful, realistic conception of justice could still be based on a closed, single-state structure was already anachronistic in 1971, when Rawls's book was first published; it makes no sense at all today, in the era of "globalization," especially for the generally small individual countries (Russia being the main exception to this) in the part of the world that we are discussing. (Meanwhile, Rawls himself has drastically reduced the scope of his original claims to universality, increasingly emphasizing, instead, their putative applicability only within a certain type of worldview—"political liberalism"—but that is another story, already noted in chapter 4, which need not concern us here. The same may be said of his effort to deal with the international arena in his relatively recent essay "The Law of Peoples."[17]) If one were simply to ask an average citizen of any country in Eastern Europe whether the ancien régime was a just one, I suspect that almost everyone would respond negatively, even the many[18] who believe that the present state of affairs is on the whole worse than the past and/or that they themselves are worse off than in the past. But this awareness of the injustices of the past hardly amounts, of course, to an endorsement of the present state of affairs as a just society, which would be utterly absurd. Not only is there the widespread domestic profiteering and opportunism bordering on and often crossing over into serious corruption that I have been depicting as commonplace in the new order, but there is also a very patent, though not easily articulable, atmosphere of being subordinate within the global context—an atmosphere of, to adapt further Iris Young's adaptation of a notion developed by the Bulgarian expatriate in France, Julia Kristeva, *abjection*.

One of the additional serious deficiencies of Rawls's and many other contemporary philosophical approaches to the value of justice is, as Young[19] and others have noted, that they are deliberately focused almost exclusively on justice in the *distribution of goods* and hence exhibit insensitivity to other dimensions of the concept of justice that may be equally or more important. It is true that Rawls does deal (almost as an afterthought) with what he calls "the problem of envy,"[20] but this notion, which is close to that of *ressentiment* mentioned earlier, does not accurately express the phenomenon to which I am now referring, either. To put the matter bluntly and, I hope, provocatively as it applies to Eastern Europe, there is a widespread, in some countries almost universal, feeling of having been on the "wrong" side in the Cold War era and of now needing to follow and imitate the victors—the United States and Western Europe—as much as possible. At the same time, and always to varying degrees in different countries, living standards are far below the standards of the West, or at least of that large, relatively prosperous part of the populations of Western countries with which the ubiquitous media offer contact, and this of course reinforces the feeling of having been on the wrong side.

If this were the whole story, then the social attitude or atmosphere to which I am pointing could indeed be understood as simply the result of highly unequal distribution, which philosophers who consider vast imbalances in goods ownership at the global level to be unfair and unjust would regard as a problem, whereas theorists in the Hayekian-Nozickian traditions would dismiss it with a *"tant pis."* But the fact is that the often vivid feeling of being regarded and treated as inferior by the West exists along with, and to some extent independently of, the condition of relative poverty of Eastern European nations; this feeling is well founded, and I wish to strongly urge that the state of affairs that occasions it is one of profound injustice. In certain respects it antedates the present era by centuries, of course, but the events both before and since 1989 have reinforced it and have given it multiple new dimensions. These dimensions cannot, I reiterate, be fully comprehended under the rubric of economic (goods) distribution; they are cultural and, in the widest sense, spiritual in nature. They amount to practices of treating the people of the region in question as abject.

These attitudes and practices are brought home in a great many ways; a couple of illustrations will clarify what I mean. There is, for instance, the widely reported condescension and disdain with which West European and American consular officials often (not always, to be sure) treat citizens of these countries who apply for visas to travel abroad, and the similar or greater disdain with which customs officials often treat those who do manage to obtain such visas. Such treatment is officially sanctioned, moreover, by such documents and legal measures as the notorious "Schengen" accord among the core countries of Western Europe that (while reducing customs barriers within the participating countries) "blacklists" citizens of certain East European countries as highly suspect if they wish to travel to the West, putting them in the same category as citizens of many "Third World" countries. (There is obviously a double racism involved here: a racism of Western Europe toward the poorer countries of Eastern Europe on the one hand, and an anger within the latter countries based on a racist feeling of superiority vis-à-vis people of the "Third World," on the other.)[21]

A second illustration of practices of abjection is to be found in commercial advertising that in effect proclaims the cultural superiority of Western, especially American, business enterprises, popular music, popular icons, and so on. The "Coca-Cola culture," as it has been called, utilizes its vast resources to popularize itself and the mass-consumption type of social ideal for which it stands as the epitome of all that is most up-to-date and most desirable, while treating local cultural artifacts and folkways with disdain, or at best as a joke. I personally observed the erection of an enormous Coca-Cola bottle, two stories high, in front of the main building of the Heritage Museum in Saint Petersburg, the former Winter Palace, as part of a sports promotion. I used this "happening," along with the photograph that I took of it, as the starting point of a paper that I gave at a conference entitled "In the Labyrinth of Culture" that was held in Saint Petersburg a year later. It seemed to me, who had regarded the scene as outrageous, an excellent case to use to attack American and general Western hegemony.[22]

This narrative has always evoked interestingly and radically different reactions from others. (A colleague of mine who teaches Russian and to whom I had given an enlarged copy of my photograph has experienced this diversity of reactions when showing it to her students, for instance.) To some, the promotion that I have described seems simply amusing, and to some it even seems highly appropriate, given the central role that the Winter Palace played in the Bolshevik Revolution of 1917 and the widely felt present need to disparage and mock everything that is reminiscent of that era. It is clear to everyone, in any case, that the widespread hegemony of the "Coca-Cola culture" is based in no small measure on a generational appeal—to the young and to all those, of whatever age, who wish to feel "with it" along with the young. Advertising is geared to make just such an appeal. And in Eastern Europe, just because of the history of the past fifty- (or, in the case of Russia, eighty-) odd years, the impulse for the younger generation to repudiate everything associated with their parents' and grandparents' time is especially strong. All of this raises the question as to whether what I have called abjection—the (alleged) infliction, on the societies in question, of massive sociocultural injustices that are not entirely reducible to the unequal distribution of goods—ought really to be seen in the light in which I have been depicting it. After all, if so many members of the societies in question accept aspects of the hegemonic culture and find it exciting and appealing, where is the injustice?

Now, it would in fact be a serious mistake to think that the peoples of Eastern Europe as a whole, especially those that have not yet been accorded the "privilege" (as it is regarded by apparent majorities in some countries) of being invited to join NATO, are unaware of the painfully subordinate, patronized position in which, objectively speaking, they find themselves today vis-à-vis the West. The recognition of this relation is quite independent of the liking that many of them may have for, say, a particular soft drink or a particular cartoon character or American films on television. Moreover, the situation as I have been describing it is, far from being an idiosyncratic interpretation of the facts, an overwhelmingly real phenomenon in today's world, even if (as is probably true) there are those who refuse to recognize it for what it is: a dominance-subordination relationship that permeates vast areas of daily life. (Someone attempting to give a more comprehensive account of it might do well to begin with the hegemony of the English language, a hegemony that has been formally recognized even by the European Community of Western Europe, to say nothing of its prevalence in the worlds of commerce, air transport, etc.) Whether "injustice" is a good name for it is no doubt more debatable, but in any case it can surely be called inequality, and I wish to suggest that any unequal, dominant-subordinate social relationship, whether large-scale or small-scale, that is not based on a generally agreed-upon difference in intrinsic ability between the two parties (such as a parent's necessarily unequal relationship to his or her small child) should properly be considered unjust. Moreover, the existence of this widespread condition of real and felt "abjection" goes a long way toward explaining, or so it seems to me, the cynicism concerning justice, both its feasibility and its very meaning, that I have found to be so widespread, even while assertions that the current situation is *un*just are frequently heard. I concur with this seemingly paradoxical attitude: I see no logical incompatibility between denying that "justice" can be either attained or even accorded a meaning that could ever attract widespread agreement, on the one hand, and making putatively objective claims concerning the existence of actual instances of injustice, on the other.[23]

Our inquiries into freedom, "traditional values," efficiency-for-profit, revenge, and finally injustice within the new order having concluded somewhat pessimistically, it may be good to return and confront directly *as values* two of the most important valued institutions and/or sets of practices, already mentioned in chapter 2, that have been most widely vaunted by those who have hoped for the best out of the changes of 1989 and since: democracy and civil society. Earlier in this chapter I called attention, with some embarrassment over feeling obliged to do so, to the highly undemocratic nature of most capitalist enterprises, at least with respect to a major portion of their memberships, the workers. (One might also do well to question the amount of democracy that exists in most such enterprises with respect to the majority of their stockholders, but that would take us too far afield.) There is, consequently, a considerable amount of hypocrisy involved in the joint promotion, so common on the part of American and West European (as well as, today, many Eastern European) ideologues, of democracy *with* capitalism. But even if we set aside, temporarily, this very crucial question of democracy in the workplace and concentrate simply on democracy as a *political* idea and set of institutions, we find that things are still not nearly so simple as these ideologues would have it. It is easy to forget now that, as I have already mentioned, a number of the old regimes included "democratic" as a word in their official self-descriptions (e.g., the "German Democratic Republic," DDR), but it is not so easy to disregard the fact that "democracy" as practiced by more recent wearers of that label in Eastern Europe has often come to mean such clearly undesirable things as political chaos—the proliferation, for example, of large numbers of political parties[24] with little commitment to working together, even in crisis situations, for something like a "common good"—and corrupt practices. As a consequence (in part) of this, the percentages of participation in a number of recent elections in Eastern European countries have fallen, in many cases, even below the typically low levels for which the United States is so justly famous. It is not that the pure *ideal* of democracy, with its modern connotations of freedom and self-determination as exercised by people, forming a community of some kind, who treat each other respectfully as equals and with tolerance for diverse points of view, is widely scorned, although of course there are those who, from various perspectives, reject it. It is simply that the practices of so many of those who proclaim the general ideal are so far removed from it that cynicism is the only reasonable response.

The problematic nature of "actually existing democracy" becomes even clearer when questions begin to be raised about the *parameters* of the "community," as I have expressed it, on behalf of which democratic ideals are being proclaimed. The problem to which I am alluding is quite obvious if we consider the case of Bosnia-Herzegovina in former Yugoslavia, where the vast majority of the population voted in the first general election with multiple parties for the respective principal parties of the three dominant ethnic groups[25] that defined it. Each of these parties was resolutely separatist, although they worked together briefly, in the first parliament following that election, under the aegis of a common desire for separation! Soon, as everyone knows, the newly independent country entered a terrible period of civil war, provoked in large measure by the fears of ethnic Serbs within Bosnia, who had formerly been citizens of a larger, multiethnic federation in which Serbs had played a rather dominant role, that they would be the objects of severe discrimination within the new order. Thus the "democratic" wishes of a clear majority of these individuals were not, by the very nature of the situation, taken seriously into account by the Western governments, beginning with Germany, which insisted on a quick recognition of the new Bosnian state. The conflict broke out very soon thereafter. The question here is not, as far as I am concerned, whether the early leadership of these people, the Bosnian Serbs, among which the name of Radovan Karadžić is foremost, was attractive or even, in a loose sense, sane; I personally believe that it was not. But the fact is that in Bosnia the implementation of supposedly routine "democratic" procedures, beginning with elections, was a major factor in producing consequences that only a fanatical misanthrope could regard as positive.[26]

Finally, with respect to democracy, there is good reason for the peoples of most, if not all, Eastern European countries, even Russia, to believe that the policies that will be carried out by their political leaderships, however scrupulous may be the adherence to "democratic" procedures in the electoral processes themselves, will in any event coincide only occasionally and, as it were, by accident with policies that a majority of them would actually favor. Part of the reason for this is the normal slippage, common to all representative governments to a greater or lesser extent, between the intentions of the electors at time t and the actions taken by the individual(s) whom they have elected for a certain time period once the latter assume office. Such normal slippage, it is important to note, is not always the result of deceitfulness and bad faith on the part of elected officials. It also arises, often enough, from changing circumstances and/or changing perceptions honestly reached.[27] In the present East European context, however, officials themselves have only very limited freedom to make major decisions in many of the most important areas of national life, since economic and economy-related policy decisions (a range that, as Karl Marx would have been the first to point out, potentially encompasses virtually all that there is to be decided!) are in fact formulated and directed in large measure by the international banking organizations and, to a lesser extent, Soros-controlled and other nongovernmental foundations. Of course, as I have often stressed, these organizations, particularly the Open Society Foundation, loudly proclaim a commitment to democracy as one of their primary goals if not their very raison d'être, and no doubt many of their officials are convinced of the truth of this. But this in no way negates the fact that they possess *and regularly exercise* vast decision-making powers that are unavailable to either the *demoi* or their elected officialdom in Eastern Europe. This state of affairs, historically unprecedented in its scope, makes a mockery of talk of political democracy in the sense of genuine self-determination in the countries in question and renders more plausible than ever, at least on the political level, the frequently encountered fatalistic attitude of "Que faire?"

But there is (as has often been said, especially in the years since 1989) a level other and "deeper" than the political, namely, the civil society. In chapter 2, I discussed the difficulty of defining what this term really means and the sense in which reference to it has constituted, particularly in the context of East European intellectual life, a repudiation of certain key ideas of Marx and of some of the totalitarian aspects of the anciens régimes. Civil society does indeed name a value or nexus of values in that part of the world. But in the current atmosphere of what I have called "abjection," cultural as well as political, it is highly doubtful that the appeal to civil society in the sense of a *local* or *regional* culture carries much weight. Of course there now exist numerous small business enterprises that would have been illicit before 1989. (The question as to whether privately owned economic enterprises should be regarded as parts of civil society, as I am treating them here, or rather as a third category in addition to the state and civil society "proper"[28] is a subordinate and largely definitional one.) Although the existence of such businesses is not unimportant, no one concerned with the flourishing of civil societies would consider this phenomenon to be adequate proof that the most valued aspects of civil society—voluntary associations operating independently of governments with the aim of promoting aspects of cultural life at local and regional levels—were being safeguarded and enhanced.

In fact, the larger picture is not very encouraging from the standpoint of those who, rightly in my view, see the institutions of civil society as a bulwark against "totalitarianism," construed in the broad sense of hegemonic domination of individuals' lives by outside influences that they have little or no role in shaping. For in the most "abject" nation-state victims of the sweeping changes that have occurred since 1989, such as Bulgaria, most local business enterprises are greatly overshadowed, in size and importance, by the transnational corporations that control advertising resources and are limited in their expansion only by the limitations (which are substantial) on what profits they can realize from impoverished local populations.[29] Meanwhile, this same impoverishment renders difficult, for all but the wealthy minority, the maintenance of some of the most basic elements of civility, such as socializing in restaurants or inviting guests to one's home, which were in some countries much more commonplace during Communist years.[30] Under these conditions it is almost taken for granted, in many circles, that anyone with an opportunity to leave the homeland to live in "the West" will, or would, of course do so. In such an atmosphere, pride in and commitment to the local cultural and other traditions that constitute the preconditions for a robust civil society are at best sporadic rather than widespread. Even in the better-off societies of the former Soviet Bloc, whereas the enforced "proletarian internationalism" of former times clearly did not succeed in destroying the local national cultures (even if we were to assume, in a manner that I regard as greatly exaggerated if not downright counterfactual for nations other than certain republics of the former Soviet Union itself, that such destruction was its aim), the conformist pressures emanating from transnational corporations and the hegemonic global culture to submerge the institutions of civil society are enormous.

In this situation as I have described it, "virtue" is indeed, again *pace* MacIntyre, an archaism. Even "value" in any noneconomic sense[31] is a notion with relatively little significance or presence. The most salient values of the recent past have collapsed, and centuries of indoctrination by tribal leaders, churchmen, politicians, and complicitous philosophers to the effect that the dominant values, whichever they may have been at any given time, were preordained and given in the nature of things, have left many people today still unprepared to accept the difficult truth that human values are nothing more nor less than human creations. Nietzsche, who dealt so interestingly with the question of transvaluing values, very accurately said that human beings would rather will the void than not will.[32] Indeed, suicide rates in much of Eastern Europe are very high, as are such suicide substitutes as heavy cigarette, alcohol, and drug consumption. I see at least three purportedly more promising alternative domains: nationalism, religious spirituality, and intense interpersonal relations. I do not wish to present these domains as mutually exclusive. Many have turned to them in the search for some sense of "higher" purpose, of sustainable value, beyond daily existence in Eastern Europe at the end of the second millennium. In fact, as I shall argue with a *soupçon* of optimism in chapter 6, all three of these proposed answers to the loss of other values have some positive as well as obvious negative aspects and interpretations.

Notes

1. Alasdair MacIntyre, *After Virtue* (Notre Dame, Ind.: University of Notre Dame Press, 1981).

2. Karl Marx and Friedrich Engels, *The German Ideology* (Moscow: Progress, 1976).

3. Leon Trotsky, *Their Morals and Ours* (New York: Pioneer, 1939).

4. *Living with Contradictions* is a title component of feminist books by Angela Barron McBride (subtitle *A Married Feminist*; New York: Harper Colophon, 1977) and Alison Jaggar, ed. (subtitle *Controversies in Feminist Social Ethics*; Boulder: Westview, 1994), but the relevance of the idea extends far beyond even the vital area of gender relations in contemporary life.

5. I am thinking of, among other events, the ousting of certain liberal analytic philosophers from the humanities faculty of the University of Zadar in Split, an action against which the Committee on International Cooperation of the American Philosophical Association lodged a protest, and the infamous attack on five Croatian feminists—Jelena Louvrić, Rada Iveković, Slavenka Drakulić, Vesna Kesić, and Dubravka Ugrešić—that was epitomized in the infamous newspaper headline and accompanying story, "Hrvatske Feministice Siluju Hrvatsku!" (Croatian feminists rape Croatia!), *Globus*, 11 December 1992, 33–34.

6. I am referring, of course, to the very influential book by "economist-king" Milton Friedman, *Capitalism and Freedom* (Chicago: University of Chicago Press, 1962).

7. Much of this antipathy, of course, has precapitalist roots. To cite an extreme and now often forgotten example, the Church officially condemned the core capitalist practice of "usury," meaning the charging of any interest at all (and not merely excessive interest) for monetary loans, until approximately a century ago, although by that time most Church members had abandoned this position in practice.

8. For a comparatively recent treatment of this, see *Marxism and Spirituality: An International Anthology*, ed. Benjamin B. Page (Westport, Conn.: Bergin and Garvey, 1993), and my review of it in *Radical Philosophy Review of Books* 9 (1994): 51–55.

9. Anecdotal evidence of this evolution, obtained from a layperson of my acquaintance who once worked on a papal commission to help formulate Church positions less critical of capitalism than some of those of the past, is confirmed by a perusal of the collection of excerpts from John Paul II's letters and speeches entitled *Agenda for the Third Millennium*, trans. A. Neame (London: HarperCollins, 1996). One might compare his remarks there "on the sig-

nificance and interpretation of capitalism" (pp. 163–67), made to a group of Verona businessmen in 1988, which begin by acknowledging "the fundamental and positive role of business, the market, [and] private property" while going on to express concern about capitalism's future global influence, with the much greater disillusionment with the capitalist system that is evident in some (chronologically) later excerpts in this volume, as well as in some remarks that he made during his visit to Cuba in early 1998.

10. He was, for instance, as Karol Wojtyła, the author of an interesting work in the tradition of what might be called phenomenological Thomism, *The Acting Person*, trans. A. Patocki, *Analecta Husserliana* 10 (Dordrecht: D. Reidel, 1979); he has also published a collection entitled *Toward a Philosophy of Praxis: An Anthology* (New York: Crossroad, 1981).

11. The spectacle of numerous prostitutes soliciting over a number of kilometers in southern Hungary on the highway leading to the border with Yugoslavia is one that I personally witnessed in 1996. Lazar Popov has reported that a similar situation obtained in 1997 on the road between his Bulgarian city, Sandanski, and the Greek border. He has also informed me of a poll taken among adolescent girls in a Bulgarian orphanage in which a plurality listed prostitution as their preferred future career choice—telling evidence of severe economic deprivation.

12. One such occasion that is especially memorable, so to speak, to me was an international conference, "Philosophiata pred Predizvikatelstvata na Promenite" (philosophy confronting the challenges of change), that was held in Sofia, Bulgaria, on October 25–26, 1997, in honor of Paul Ricoeur. Ricoeur himself focused on the theme of collective memory, insisting that historical memory was both peculiarly prevalent and peculiarly problematic in *Europe*, an assertion to which I was not prepared to assent wholeheartedly. A certain segment of the Bulgarian participants, notably Mikhail Nedelchev, went so far as to claim that it was impossible to have a dialogue with former Communists except concerning the errors of the past. It is obviously true that, absent all memory, there is no longer a human personality; but it is also true, as a psychological statement of fact, that selective forgetting can have a therapeutic effect—for groups and nations, no doubt, as well as for individuals.

An excellent discussion of aspects of the Bulgarian situation in this regard is that of Lilyana Deyanova, "The Battles for the Mausoleums (Traumatic Places of the Collective Memory)," in *Bulgaria at the Crossroads*, ed. Jacques Coenen-Huther (New York: Nova Science Publishers, 1996), 175–86.

13. For an interesting journalistic discussion of some of the recent general literature on these issues, see Timothy Garton Ash, "The Truth about Dictatorship," *New York Review of Books*, 19 February, 1998, 35–40. Ash omits philosophers from his initial list of types of individuals who might have something to say on these issues, and so it is unsurprising that he combines precise and often valuable historical details with vagueness and imprecision at the conceptual level (e.g., in his apparent assumption that the words "dictatorship" and "democracy" are more or less self-explanatory). One of the results of this is that he accepts with very little hesitation the dubious premise, which is shared by

some of the authors and editors of the literature under review, that the case of post-Communist Eastern Europe is comparable, with very few adjustments or qualifications, to the cases of certain Latin American countries that were until recently characterized by regimes relying heavily on paramilitary "death squads," as well as to those of South Africa and even of post-Franco Spain and post-Hitler Germany. Such vast attempted generalizations, which unfortunately also characterize some of the nascent philosophical literature on these topics, seem to me excessively facile and unhelpful for understanding the East European situation.

14. There is, to be sure, a vast philosophical as well as religious literature on the topic of forgiveness, but I regard the most impressive account of its role in overcoming hypocritical hard-heartedness and paving the way for the possibility of genuine human community to be Hegel's treatment of it in the final pages of the section entitled "Conscience: The 'beautiful soul:' Evil and the Forgiveness of It" in his *Phenomenology of Mind*, trans. J. B. Baillie, 2d ed. (London: George Allen & Unwin; New York: Macmillan, 1961), 668–79. Though expressed in very difficult language, it reflects the forgiving attitudes of many ordinary people as well as *some* intellectuals with respect to the misdeeds, real and alleged, of the past, absent which the future can consist of nothing but strife.

15. John Rawls, *A Theory of Justice* (Cambridge: Harvard University Press, 1971), 3.

16. Rawls, *A Theory of Justice*, 8.

17. John Rawls, "The Law of Peoples," *Critical Inquiry* 20 (autumn 1993): 36–68. A brief but valuable critique of certain aspects of this essay is to be found in Jeffrey R. Paris, "Impossible Hope: New Critical Theory and the Spirit of Liberation" (Ph.D. diss., Purdue University, 1998), 71–75.

18. Some polls in Bulgaria, for example, have shown up to 90 percent concurrence in the proposition that those polled are worse off, economically speaking, than before; economic statistics more or less confirm this popular impression.

19. Iris Marion Young, *Justice and the Politics of Difference* (Princeton: Princeton University Press, 1990).

20. Rawls, *Theory of Justice,* 530–34.

21. From the recent explosion of philosophical literature on racism, particularly in the United States, I would like to cite three especially valuable books: *Exploitation and Exclusion: Race and Class in Contemporary US Society*, ed. Abebe Zegeye, Leonard Harris, and Julia Maxted (Borough Green, Kent: Hans Zell, 1991); Lewis Gordon, *Bad Faith and Antiblack Racism* (Atlantic Highlands: Humanities Press, 1995); and *Overcoming Racism and Sexism*, ed. Linda A. Bell and David Blumenfeld (Lanham, Md.: Rowman & Littlefield, 1995). But all of them are geared toward American audiences above all, and hence say little about European conditions.

Aware as I have been of the devastating psychological and personal effects of the Schengen accords on Bulgarians, for whom this agreement has made travel to Western Europe extremely difficult even when they do have the funds needed for such a trip, I came across a letter from a middle-class Frenchman concerning the extremely humiliating procedures that he and his family had to undergo in order to bring his mother-in-law over from Haiti to visit with her daughter (a naturalized French citizen) and her grandchildren: a forty-five-day waiting period involving even a precise measurement of his home, as well as numerous financial statements, before she was permitted to receive a stamp in her passport, not from the French government but from the "Etats Schengen." The implementation of this agreement is an obvious symptom of the dramatic diminution of the old nation-state sovereignties in Western Europe, as the letter writer points out, and this is a fact of which at least some Americans are aware; but its racist aspects, which are unquestionable, are not yet widely known in the United States. Didier Charlemagne, "'L'honneur de désobéir'" [citing an earlier article], *Le Monde Diplomatique*, October 1997, 2.

22. McBride, "Coca-Cola Culture and Other Cultures: Against Hegemony," in *In Labyrinth of Culture*, ed. Liubava Moreva (Saint Petersburg, Russia, Centre Eidos, 1997), 154–68; a revised version is to appear in *Relativism: Science, Religion, and Philosophy*, ed. Chandana Chakrabarti (Lanham, Md.: Rowman & Littlefield, in press).

23. I argue for this position in "Social Justice on Trial: The Verdict of History," *Analecta Husserliana* 31 (1990): 159–68.

24. Given the fact that former Yugoslavia was divided into six republics, the largest of which included two autonomous regions, and that in each of these entities a number of parties came into existence at the time of change, it was estimated that at one time there were over one hundred formally recognized political parties in that country. No other country of which I am aware approached that order of magnitude, but the general fact of proliferation was, and to some extent remains, widespread.

25. It should not be forgotten that Sarajevo at that time also included a small but significant Jewish community, a sizable number of persons, many of "mixed" parentage, who formally listed their nationality as "Yugoslav" rather than Serb, Croat, or Muslim, and, of course, some individuals from other parts of the nationality spectrum as it then existed in Yugoslavia: Albanians, Slovenians, and so on.

26. Hegel, of course, no democrat but also no fanatical misanthrope, argued for the positive value of war from the standpoint of world history. But I cannot imagine that even he would have found much to endorse in the civil war in Bosnia. It is, however, true that a leading government minister of the "Serbian Republic" portion of Bosnia had been a teacher of Hegel in the Philosophy Department of the University of Sarajevo before the war began.

Certain elements within Serbia have made the point that, in the face of all counter-currents, that country has retained a nominally socialist constitution, which fact, they have argued, should win applause from the Left in other countries. But, as I have pointed out to them on more than one occasion, when the Left in other countries considers former Yugoslavia, it tends to see first and foremost the phenomenon of a brutal and devastating war, by contrast with which most other phenomena seem relatively unimportant.

27. Jean-Jacques Rousseau, proponent of popular sovereignty, goes much further than this when he says, famously, "The English people thinks it is free. It greatly deceives itself; it is free only during the election of the members of Parliament. As soon as they are elected, it is a slave, it is nothing." *On the Social Contract* 3, 15, trans. Roger D. and Judith R. Masters (New York: St. Martin's, 1978), 102. As Roger Masters points out in his editor's note, 149, Rousseau attempted to deal with the practical impossibility of direct democracy in large modern states by proposing, in his model but never implemented constitution for Poland, that deputies be required to follow their electors' instructions. This strikes me as unsound.

28. Jürgen Habermas claims that there has been a movement from conceiving of civil society in terms especially of economic structures, as it was in Hegel and Marx, to this tripartite distinction among state, economic sphere, and civil society. He ties this alleged evolution to his own increased use of the term *Zivilgesellschaft* instead of the old *"bürgerliche Gesellschaft."* See his *Faktizität und Geltung: Beiträge zur Diskurstheorie des Rechts und des demokratischen Rechtsstaats* (Frankfurt am Main: Suhrkamp, 1992), 443. I am not qualified to comment on the evolution of the meanings of terms in the German language, but I do not consider the sharp separation between the economic sphere and civil society to be a conceptually useful development.

29. See my paper "Clarifying 'Civil Society' and Creating Space for Civil Societies: From the Struggle against Nation-State Despotisms to the Critique of Despotic Transnationalisms," in *Resurrecting the Phoenix: Proceedings from the International Conference on Civil Society in South East Europe: Philosophical and Ethical Perspectives*, ed. David C. Durst, Maria Dimitrova, Alexander Gungov, and Borislava Vassileva (Sofia: EOS, 1998).

30. This is a universal, commonplace assertion in Bulgaria today, for example.

31. Jean-Paul Sartre, whose various subtle treatments of values, so far removed from much of both the traditional and contemporary standard philosophical discussions that, problematically, take for granted the existence of something like an "ethical domain" and confine themselves to attempting precisely to delineate its contours, has written a little noticed but very illuminating analysis of diverse meanings of this word "in the *ethical* sense." He begins this discussion, which appears in the form of a lengthy footnote, by asserting that the economic sense of it is, in an important way, primitive. See his *Critique of Dialectical Reason*, trans. A. Sheridan-Smith (London: NLB; Atlantic Highlands: Humanities, 1976), 247–50. See also my discussion of it in *Sartre's Political Theory* (Bloomington: Indiana University Press, 1991), 135–37.

32. Friedrich Nietzsche, *On the Genealogy of Morals*, trans. W. Kaufmann (New York: Vintage, 1967), 163.

Chapter Six

The Throne, the Altar, and the Cottage

The title of this chapter is a reordered imitation of the principal themes of a book of nineteenth-century intellectual history, Cecil Driver's *Tory Radical: The Life of Richard Oastler*.[1] That it would be relevant here, in the context of Eastern Europe at the end of our millennium, says something, I am sure, about continuity and change in history. Above all, it seems to me to speak to the fact that two hundred years are really not a very long period of time from a larger perspective. In a recent film about his life, famous octogenarian Russian academician N. N. Moiseyev recounts something his father once told him that his grandfather had said, "The Bolsheviks come and go, but Russia remains." Then Moiseyev adds, tellingly, "The democrats come and go, but Russia remains."[2] And it is not in Russia alone that such remarks are made!

Oastler was an interesting (if now forgotten) figure who deplored the increasing enchantment of his Tory Party with the then-new values of economic liberalism, values that he considered to be in stark opposition to traditional Tory values as he understood them—the altar, the throne, and the cottage. (One can imagine what his reaction to Margaret Thatcher would have been.) In the present context, it is a similar set of values—one or another or sometimes all three at once—often presented as the values, respectively, of the nation (*not* of a throne in the literal sense: I acknowledge but do not take very seriously the minority parties in certain countries of Eastern Europe that advocate the return of their tsars), the Church (Catholic, Orthodox, Muslim, or Protestant, as the case may be), and the family, which are being proposed as solutions to the current crisis of values in the part of the world that we are considering. I shall try to reflect on the meanings and possible relevance of each in turn, suggesting in each case what of positive value might be extracted from it.

Nationalism, Pride in National Cultures, and Cosmopolitanism

In the past decade local nationalism has enjoyed a resurgence of an often sinister sort that would have seemed highly improbable to many scholars a few years earlier. In fact, anyone who had spent some time in former Yugoslavia and had been attentive to people's attitudes would have been aware that national identity (as Serb, Croat, etc., or even, as the line in passports indicating a citizen's "nationality" permitted and a small percentage always wrote, "Yugoslav") was considered a highly significant and often sensitive fact there. A similar situation obtained in the Soviet Union itself, where, however, a policy of minimizing or simply suppressing national identities (other than Russian) was more often pursued by the central government than in the case of former Yugoslavia. (The treatment of the Albanian majority in Kosovo in recent years is the most blatant counterexample to this generalization.) Moreover, within the countries of the Soviet Bloc itself it was well known that pride in national identity, particularly in countries such as Poland and Hungary with centuries-long histories of resistance to Russian encroachments, was an important rallying point in opposition to Soviet hegemony. Nevertheless, in spite of all of these well-known facts, the strength and virulence of some nationalist revivals took many of the supposed experts by surprise.

If we make an exception for the case of Chechnya and the struggle between Azerbaijan and Armenia over the Nagorno-Karabakh region (in technical geographical terms the Transcaucasus is a part of Europe, although this fact is seldom mentioned, in my experience, in discussions of Eastern Europe), the most obvious examples of virulent nationalism in the part of the world that we are considering are of course those from former Yugoslavia. The nationalist-based tensions and ensuing conflicts there have, unlike many other developments in Eastern Europe, received considerable mention in Western media and popular literature, and superficial explanations abound. The most popular, no doubt, is "revival of ancient tribal antagonisms," or words to similar effect. "Those people," in other words, are just that way, having been brought up from childhood to hate their ethnically distinct neighbors. What is philosophically interesting about this shamelessly superficial attitude is its implicit theory of inherited ethnic identity and, once again, the contempt that it displays toward the "abject" peoples under discussion.

So how possibly *can* we explain what happened? I can briefly summarize my own perception of the tragic sequence of events in former Yugoslavia, which I happen to have visited twice within two months of the breakup of the Yugoslav Federation and the ensuing hostilities, by observing that few knowledgeable, trained academic observers of the situation, with several of whom I actually spoke at the time, expected it to evolve in quite so violent a way as it did; thus, the allocation of blame needs to be diffuse. A comprehensive explanation should include the following: the role played by certain politicians who inflamed public opinion for reasons of perceived personal advantage; the part played, for example, by the newly liberated press, eager to sell copy by proliferating atrocity charges concerning both the recent and the distant past; the role of Western governments, which both failed to take action when it would have been advisable and then interfered in ways that were ill advised and counterproductive; and even, as I noted in chapter 5, some of the questionable ways in which "democracy" was interpreted and "democratic" procedures were implemented. To pursue this task of historical explanation with the depth that it merits, however, would take us rather far away from our present focus, which is nationalism considered as a possible value; it would, moreover, involve considerable repetition of work that has already been done reasonably well, or at least begun.[3]

We should not allow the closeness of the horrendous Yugoslav example of the sociopolitical uses to which nationalism has been put to cause us to forget other examples, some equally or even more horrendous, but some less so. German nationalism and, at least in the First World War, French counternationalism were central ingredients in the most massive officially sanctioned slaughters of this waning century, and there are a number of instances of political nationalism at work in less sanguinary, even if often problematic, forms throughout the world today, including other parts of Eastern Europe. (There was, for instance, the peaceful breakup of former Czechoslovakia into two nations; there are the repressive, but generally not genocidal, nationalist measures being undertaken against ethnic Russians in some of the Baltic and other former republics of the USSR; etc.) But exactly what is the meaning of this word, "nationalism," that is uttered so glibly and usually, among *bien pensants* intellectuals at least, with such horror—for example, by American political scientists who may in the very same breath insist on the importance of promoting American values throughout the world? Despite (and in part because of) a fairly extensive literature on the topic, it remains elusive.

Modern genetics has rather decisively put pay to the possibility of rationally defending the racist versions of nationalism that are still so popular everywhere. There is no decisive way of demarcating various ethnicities along biological lines, and in fact that is hardly a surprise if we consider the multiethnic origins of virtually all peoples. Centuries of intermarriage among the various groups of former Yugoslavia and with neighboring groups, for example, render quite illusory the idea that it might be possible to identify a "pure" Serbian or Croatian type, while at the same time anyone living in either of these countries is aware of the existence of significant regional differences in dialect, customs, and so on, from one part of them to another. Clearly, national identity is something that has been socially, historically forged. This fact has led some writers to speak in terms of "imagined communities"[4] and seekers of consensus to urge delinkage of nationalism from the nation-state in the name of the rule of constitutionalism and law.[5] An excessively cerebral approach to the issue, however, misses the point of what really lies behind the sort of nationalism that has produced the atrocities of recent years, namely, a deep visceral appeal, in significant ways similar to and sometimes directly linked with sexual desire and various addictions. This has been well captured by Natalija Mićunović in her doctoral dissertation, "A Critique of Nationalism," based on the Serbian experience.[6] The "high" that comes from feeling oneself to be a part of a group in contrast with, and usually in potential if not active opposition to, other groups cannot be underestimated. A nation is no doubt the largest such group that is readily conceivable in our present world, except for the "high" that is probably experienced by some of the moviegoers who flock to films portraying us earth dwellers as under siege from extraterrestrial aliens.

This way of viewing nationalist urges of the sort that can generate outrages such as those of which we have heard all too much in recent years shows them to be manifestations of something fundamental about being human—about human projects, human desires—and might be taken to imply a pessimistic conclusion concerning their eliminability. But this conclusion is no more warranted than the conclusion that it is utterly impossible to overcome a drug addiction because some drug addictions are so strong. But the intended object of any nationalism, even the most straightforward and simple-minded, is far more complicated and consists of far more elements than is any addiction to a single drug. Since, as I have argued, every nationalism is a human construct, involving a certain set of values, rather than a physiological given, it should therefore always be possible, in principle, to "reconstruct" it in such a way as to suppress its more malign features and retain those features, if there are any, that can serve a positive function.

It seems plausible to me to say that in today's world, and specifically in today's Eastern Europe, some such positive features do indeed survive. There is no gainsaying the attractiveness of what my colleague, Martin Beck Matuštík, calls "postnational identity,"[7] rooted in an existentialist sense of freedom, inwardness, and transcendence, to which one finds, as he shows, valuable pointers in the works of Kierkegaard in the nineteenth century and of Václav Havel himself in our time. It must nevertheless be recognized, as numerous commentators on "post-Marxism" and "postmodernism" have remarked, that whatever is presented as "post-x" must by definition still retain a reference to the "x." It must still, in other words, be a transitional standpoint inasmuch as what has been left behind is still remembered and still plays a role. Historical memories of national identities of the past—of one's ancestors' ways of life and historical experiences—can include both terrible aspects (such as the massacres at the end of World War II and in earlier times that were recalled by the various nationalist presses in the prelude to the war in former Yugoslavia) and enriching ones (such as music and other cultural artifacts). In either case they can be interpreted and put to present use in the most diverse ways. (For example, the words "Never again!" can be spoken in a wide variety of tones and with a view to a vast range of possible attitudes and actions.) All of this reminds us that the sort of "nationalism" which consists in taking a pride in one's national culture need not find ultimate expression in bellicosity and hostile competition. It can instead serve as an important component, for some individuals perhaps the most important component, of the activities and institutions of civil society. At least this much can be said, then, for nationalism's potential positive aspects at the present time.

However, the countries of Eastern Europe today constantly exist in the shadow, as I have repeatedly asserted, of a certain kind of "*trans*nationalism," that is, the financial dominance and cultural hegemony of the great transnational corporations and of the Western economic and political entities in which they are based and with which they are aligned; I have elsewhere called this state of affairs "despotic transnationalism."[8] This phenomenon bears some formal resemblance to an ancient ideal that has been experiencing a heartening revival in philosophical discussions of the past several years, namely, cosmopolitanism,[9] in that both are global in scope. The cosmopolitan ideal, aimed ultimately at the abolition of nation-states and of state borders on the political level,[10] as well as at the elimination of national identity when considered as exclusionary and as the ground for hostile competition at the ethical level, does not seem to me to be incompatible with efforts to defend the continued existence of national cultures—an existence that is clearly menaced, in many cases and in many ways, by the very powerful forces to which I am referring. In fact it is these very forces which, though transnational, in effect often serve, during the present era, as the instruments of a specific nationalism that seems to me to have the potential of being the most sanguinary of all: American nationalism. At least as long as that potential endures, then alternative nationalisms will continue to have a clear raison d'être—to some extent even, unfortunately, at the political level as well as at the civil and cultural ones.

My being an "insider" within the American scene while being an outsider, albeit a comparatively well-traveled one, to Eastern Europe, may serve me in good stead in trying to understand and explain the present situation. A perceptive Bulgarian student to whom I made mention of American nationalism regarded as a menace remarked that the American character appeared to him just too diverse and relativistic to give itself over to any doctrinaire or ideological nationalism and that for such purposes, at least, relativism was not such a bad thing. I could agree with him only partially. It is true, of course, that an experimental, antidogmatic approach, no doubt better labeled "pragmatism," has enjoyed great popularity in the United States and become incorporated in a philosophical movement by that name. A self-styled contemporary version of this philosophical outlook has been popularized by Richard Rorty, whose work has been widely read and frequently translated. Rorty himself, personally as well as in his writings, appears to be quite the opposite of a doctrinaire nationalist thinker. A glance at some of his essays, however, reveals a level of satisfaction with regard to the supposed superiority of the liberal worldview with which he identifies himself that I find troubling[11] (as have others). This conviction of the superiority of the "American way of life" is another frequently found aspect of the national mentality. When endorsed by "patriots" with less benign attitudes toward others than Rorty usually displays, it has led in the past to a Crusader spirit, jingoism, and widespread bellicosity in the American public. (The outset of the Spanish-American War, at the very time when, coincidentally, the popularity of William James's original pragmatism was rising, is one good example; James himself was a pacifist and strong critic of American imperialism.[12]) The U.S. Congress seems always to have a number of members with such attitudes, constantly on the lookout for a casus belli (particularly if American "superiority," meaning in concrete terms military superiority, can be demonstrated at relatively little cost). In recent years it has come to be considered desirable for leading American diplomats (such as recent ambassadors to the United Nations) to speak with belligerence and to treat with undisguised contempt both foreign leaders who are considered "uncooperative" and even, at least by implication, the people whom they lead. And this way of conducting diplomacy is often described by admiring journalists as a good example of a "hardheaded, pragmatic approach."

Even now, such ways of thinking and behaving sometimes create dissonance within the global transnational order, as when American laws aimed at punishing foreign-based companies that attempt to do business in countries most disliked by the U.S. leadership, such as Cuba and Libya, met with stiff resistance from some of those companies and their mostly European governments. For the most part, however, American dominance of the present international political-economic order is accepted as a fact. Because American politicians are for the most part very strong boosters of that order, the transnational movers and shakers are rather content. Under these circumstances, coupled with the well-known vast military capability of the United States, I do not think that my assertion that U.S. nationalism of a potentially virulent and violent sort remains a serious threat can rightly be regarded as far-fetched.

It is this situation that will help to explain, and perhaps to some extent even to justify[13](if it should occur) an eventual resurgence, in the countries of Eastern Europe, of nationalist sentiments of a different and more dangerous sort than the benign pride in one's national culture and civil society. At present, such sentiments do not appear to me to be very widespread outside of former Yugoslavia (where they have at least temporarily waned somewhat) and parts of the former Soviet Union itself; in fact, to the contrary, there is well-documented, strong support for joining the American-dominated North Atlantic Treaty Organization in such countries as Poland and Hungary. But it is not unreasonable to anticipate a reaction against this domination at some future time.[14] The superiority of the cosmopolitan ideal over a world torn by nationalist rivalries and attempted hegemonies seems obvious to me, but I see little evidence of a commitment to this ideal within the political leadership of the world's "superpower." In the long run, of course, when all of us will be dead, an increased recognition of the full implications of the fact that our world is now *one*[15] in a far fuller sense, given postmodern technology, than at any previous historical period will lead to the intensification of new value concerns (e.g., those of an ecological sort) that will make aggressive, belligerent versions of nationalism appear even more ridiculous than they already appear to many observers today, although this eventuality by no means guarantees a "happy ending" in world history. But in the short run the place of nationalism as a complex, ambiguous locus of values and disvalues needs to be understood and, in some sense, accepted, as I hope to have shown here.

Religion and the Things of the Spirit

In a great many of the countries of Eastern Europe today there is an undoubted religious revival. As always in such matters, and perhaps even more than in most, a note of caution concerning the differences from one country to another needs to be inserted here. Nevertheless, the intended symbolism of the Russian government's having spent a vast sum of money, amid national poverty, to erect an enormous, gleaming Orthodox cathedral on a site within easy walking distance of the Kremlin, on which another cathedral had once stood before being demolished at Stalin's orders early in his reign, is entirely obvious. It reflects an important aspect of current reality that is to be found, in some form or other, virtually everywhere in the region. What is its meaning?

First, it is important to acknowledge the extent to which, now as in the past, there often exists a close linkage between "the altar" and "the throne." In divided former Yugoslavia, religious differences played a significant part in fanning the flames of war, although their role has sometimes been overemphasized and many commentators have failed in any case to recognize the degree to which resurgent local nationalisms brought about and then often used the religious revival rather than the other way around. (In both Serbia and Croatia, former Communists-turned-nationalists frequently "found religion" and started crossing themselves ostentatiously and courting church leaders for the first time in their lives, in moves of expediency that often bordered on the ludicrous. In the predominantly Muslim part of Bosnia, especially in urban areas, religious practice as such, as distinct from sheerly cultural practices of an often religious origin, had been rather minimal for many years, but events have brought about a considerable restoration of state-endorsed religious observance and religious education, to the dismay and discomfort of the non-Muslims who remain, as well as, of course, of many Muslims.[16]) In such traditionally Orthodox countries as Russia and Bulgaria, strong and at present quite successful efforts are underway to reestablish, in fact if perhaps not *eo nomine*, the Orthodox Church as a state church. In Poland, the struggle of a large part of the Catholic hierarchy and its conservative political allies to achieve a similar outcome has been an extremely divisive factor, even as the economy has begun to improve. In that country more than in perhaps any other, the Church always served as a rallying point for anti-Soviet and anti-Russian national sentiment under the old regime, and it always retained sufficient strength to force the regime to deal with it. But in virtually every country in which an overwhelming majority of the population has at least a nominal affiliation with a single religious sect, a more or less holy alliance between church and state appears to be very tempting to leaders of both and is being widely preached. As far from incidental side effects of this, religious education in the schools is widely being re-established as an option; some church leaders advocate making it a requirement. Alternative sects, especially those of a non-traditional and proselytizing sort, are threatened with suppression.

As long as we are discussing temptations, it is no doubt necessary to take note of the very powerful temptation, to which I shall not be the first to succumb, to quote Marx one more time on this subject; I refer to what must be his best-known sentence, or at least one of the two or three best-known: "Religion is the sigh of the oppressed creature, the sentiment of a heartless world, and the soul of soulless conditions; it is the opiate of the people."[17] As it has also been said more than once, the literal meaning of these words can be taken in a sense that is the opposite of the standard interpretation of their significance, which was probably Marx's own intention, namely, that they are demeaning to the claims and self-images of the great religions. After all, it can be said on the other side, for those for whom the world really appears as Marx describes it ("heartless" and "soulless") the existence of such a powerful opiate, as a substitute for the expensive drug that ordinary people cannot afford, may indeed be very welcome.

And so it surely is for many Eastern Europeans today. Officially treated like a mind-destroying drug under the anciens régimes, oppressed to varying degrees depending on the country and time period, religion always retained a somewhat ambiguous status. (Only in Albania, it would seem, was the suppression of the churches virtually absolute; elsewhere religious belief was at least generally "tolerated," however grudgingly, at a minimum as a superstition that less intelligent older people who had grown up in earlier days might unfortunately be expected to cling to, preferably only in private.[18]) This ambiguity was due in large measure to the very central role that religion had played in every country's history and tradition, phenomena that most Communist leaders recognized as easier to try to manipulate and reinterpret than to extirpate. Even if, for instance, the churches within the Kremlin walls were put to very nonreligious uses, it was impossible to pretend that they had not been churches at one time. Virtually all of the older art of Eastern Europe, like that of Western Europe during the Middle Ages, had been religious in character; and iconoclasm was not official Communist Party doctrine. Nor, despite Stalin's now avenged cathedral destruction in Moscow, was there in most places anything approaching a policy of universally demolishing church structures. Even for many thoroughly nonreligious people, these often extremely beautiful, haunting artworks and monuments are powerful reminders of an older heritage with which it would be difficult and bizarre not to feel a certain sense of pride and self-identification.

The religious ceremonies that are once again being held with general public acceptance and even approbation, rather than in the atmosphere of oppression in which they were formerly held when they were held at all, of course have additional significance beyond that of commemorating a heritage: they endorse a structure of beliefs of a philosophically relevant kind as well as a clergy that supposedly acts as guardian of those beliefs. Let us first consider the latter. The phenomenon of the clergy seems to me to pose a considerable problem, though less from a theoretical than from a practical point of view. The clergy consists of a group of men (that they are still overwhelmingly of a single sex in the countries in question is one aspect of the general issue of human relationships, especially gender relationships, to which I shall return shortly) who, for various reasons and under quite diverse circumstances depending on the period at which they made their decision, have chosen a unique career that by definition identifies them as committed to a vision of reality that is not shared by the majority of the populations almost anywhere today but evokes great admiration among some and great contempt among others. Today, the possibilities of being corrupted by the will to power are considerable for some who have climbed this career ladder high enough, and the often Byzantine (pun intended) struggle for ascendancy (in Bulgaria, for instance, the dispute as to which pretender should be considered the true Patriarch, comparable to debates over the papal succession in medieval Europe) often involves the potential control of extensive resources. All of this has very little to do with the serious concerns of any reasonable person who is considering a return to, or a renewal of, religious beliefs as a focal point of a system of viable values. Claims to papal infallibility and the existence of a somewhat more rigid command structure within the Roman Catholic clergy further complicate the situation in countries such as Poland in which nominal Catholics constitute the overwhelming majority, as compared to countries of a predominantly Orthodox "persuasion." But even in Catholic countries there is a strong countertradition of considering the religion to be ultimately the patrimony of the people rather than of the hierarchy, and believers in this tradition can often find common cause with those nonbelievers who are not excessively hostile to them. The most serious issue as far as the role of the clergy is concerned, then, seems to me to be the ever present temptation among religious and political elites to make common cause in their own self-interest. But this is a familiar question of the corruption of power, not a specifically religious question.

Religious beliefs themselves, on the other hand, are quite a different and ultimately more serious matter from both the social and the philosophical points of view. The attempt by some believers to universally enforce their religious dogmas of both ethical (e.g., the supposed absolute impermissibility of abortion under any circumstances) and, sometimes, metaphysical (e.g., monotheism, mandated as a national creed in a constitution or in a "pledge of allegiance") varieties strikes me as outrageous from both philosophical and policy perspectives, whether it occurs in the United States or in Ireland or in Poland. It obviously resembles, as many have noted, the mandating of Marxism-Leninism as official doctrine under the old regimes. The extent to which compulsory religious education may be adopted in some of the countries of Eastern Europe in the near future will be a measure of these countries' submission to a new ideological yoke.

One of the almost inevitable aspects of such mandatory religious education, if it is reinstated, will of course be the process of teaching children, depending on their exact geographical locations, that Orthodoxy is good and Roman Catholicism despicable or at least terribly confused (e.g., in Bulgaria or Serbia) or that the opposite is true (e.g., in Poland or Croatia). The test of whether this predictable sectarian teaching has any real intellectual respectability, it seems to me, must ultimately be the seriousness with which the teachers on both sides are willing to take a defensible stand on the *filioque* question which originally divided the two halves of Christendom. Within the Blessed Trinity, does the Holy Spirit (or Holy Ghost) proceed from both the Father and the Son, or from the Father only? The adherents of the former position, who insisted on inserting *filioque* (and the Son) in the official creed after the words *qui ex patre* (who from the Father) and before the word *procedit* (proceeds), are linked with Rome, their opponents with Byzantium and its heirs. I am not myself sure which formula, if either, is "true," or indeed whether the whole issue has much "real" meaning at all, although I believe I could give plausible explanations of the underlying issues as they originate in certain alternative theological assumptions within the overall framework of Christianity. But I *am* morally certain that very few would-be religious instructors of children in Eastern Europe today, despite the undoubted, widely reported sectarian partisanship of many of them, care much about it or even know very much about it and that most would regard my remarks here as a joke. If I am right about this, it seems to me to show to what extent the attempted revival of *doctrinal, sectarian* religion in the current situation is hypocritical, self-serving, and even self-contradictory rather than promising as a source of potentially important values.

But religious yearning, however much a subject of Marx's ridicule and Enlightenment-style distaste (his mother was apparently a practitioner of Jewish Orthodoxy, a religious standpoint that ill accorded with the dominant intellectual spirit of the period of his youth), not only is understandable in light of this world's ills, as the original citation from him shows that he understood, but also has its positive side when it is sufficiently detached from the clerical and dogmatic meshes within which it always risks being caught. If there is a single ideal that informs the present book, it is that of the primacy of the "spirit," of those aspects of ourselves as human that are not reducible to the decadent, soulless, profit-obsessed aspects that I have portrayed, in the previous chapter and throughout, as currently dominant. However unsuccessful *organized* religion has been in resisting this reduction, religious artifacts and rituals themselves nevertheless point the human spirit, in what are admittedly often primitive-seeming or *kitschisch* ways,[19] to realms of reality that transcend the mundane—whatever interpretation one chooses to give to the notion of "transcendence." I shall touch upon these matters again in my final chapter. Here, I am simply offering a sympathetic understanding of the return, on the part of important segments of the peoples of Eastern Europe, to the values symbolized by "the altar," while yet agreeing completely with friends who see in this trend a source of potentially great new divisiveness within the national civil societies of the region.

Family Values and Concern for Human Relationships

In Richard Oastler's trinity of values, "the cottage" referred to the sturdy English countryfolk whom he took to be the "backbone of the nation." Much of Eastern Europe today retains a large rural population, and the continued presence of parents and grandparents back in the villages of the countryside is still a powerful inducement to younger people, who inevitably move in increasing numbers to the cities, not to consider trying to leave their homelands to seek better opportunities in the West even when they might otherwise be sorely tempted to do so. In short, the family, whether rural or urban, remains a very important element of cohesion and focus of values, perhaps the least damaged of all such foci through the upheavals and radical changes of the past half-century. In addition, the tradition of mutual aid within families has been a crucial factor in preventing the economic crises that have racked the region, and continue to rack it in so many areas, from having even more catastrophic effects than they have had. Family members who own plots of land on which to grow fruits and vegetables for summer eating and winter canning have contributed greatly to the alleviation of food shortages and the avoidance of widespread malnutrition. The sharing of housing accommodations between generations helps account for the continued survival of people whose pathetically low incomes would otherwise relegate them to a status well below the poverty level. These last remarks may perhaps seem airy and overgeneralized, and of course they cannot apply equally to every country of Eastern Europe. But I am confident of their accuracy as far as Bulgaria and Russia are concerned, where the facts about salaries and food crises are very well known. I have observed families coping in the ways indicated, and I am reasonably confident that they are more widely applicable. If I seem to be avoiding more precise documentation here, it is largely out of a feeling of sympathy and respect for the privacy of friends and acquaintances whose material circumstances are, as I write this, comparatively so much worse, for reasons over which they have had no control, than they were a decade ago.

The very same circumstances that I have just noted, however, are obviously sources of great potential stress, especially when considered in conjunction with the fact that pensioners have been, as I mentioned in chapter 2, among the most adversely affected victims of government budget cutting in the name of the brave new market world. Significant portions of younger persons' salaries have had to be used to support parents and grandparents who would formerly have had sufficient retirement benefits to be more or less self-supporting. Crowded housing conditions (which were, however, common under the old regimes, as well) tend to greatly intensify feelings of hardship. This ambivalent state of affairs suggests a number of questions about the meaning and optimal form of "family values," a term that has frequently been used in demagogic and unabashedly reactionary ways by politicians in the United States and other countries. It is because of the history of this usage that I prefer to identify the domain of values that I am about to consider with the label "human relationships."

> The relation of man to woman is *the most natural* relation of human being to human being. . . . In this relationship is revealed . . . the extent to which man's *need* has become a *human* need; the extent to which, therefore, the *other* person as a person has become for him a need—the extent to which he in his individual existence is at the same time a social being.[20]

The profound truth of this observation, which in Marx's 1844 manuscript appears rather suddenly and almost as an aphorism, lies in the obvious fact that male-female relationships of dominance and subordination have constituted by far the largest single aggregate type of unjust inequality throughout human history, so that the drive to alter them in the direction of equality is the single most important key to improving human relationships as a whole. Marxist-Leninists in power in the old regimes did indeed make some conscious efforts along these lines, insisting, for example, that there be a substantial number of women delegates to party congresses and other theoretically "legislative" bodies and that women be accepted as fellow workers in industry and other modern types of employment. But, as has been pointed out many times, these policies often amounted to mere lip service, falling far short of genuine equality: by and large, the bosses of both politics and industry remained overwhelmingly male, while at the same time traditional patriarchal expectations concerning "women's work" in the home endured, little effort being made to alter them, so that the total *quantity* of work expected of the average woman probably underwent an increase in most of the societies in question.[21]

One interesting implication of this rather universally agreed upon description of the change in women's status under the old regimes seems to be that, however generally "totalitarian" the latter were, they did not on the whole succeed in entirely dominating family life (despite recorded instances of spouses spying on spouses, etc.), for otherwise the traditional expectations that I have mentioned could have come under heavier attack from the regimes than they did. The simplest explanation of their lack of wholehearted commitment to gender equality is, of course, that the men who dominated them were especially hypocritical in this domain, preferring to keep their own wives and other close female associates subordinate and not wishing to rock their domestic boats too much by insisting very loudly on the official line, which theoretically endorsed equality. This is undoubtedly true, but we should be cautious about accepting it as the *entire* explanation because then an issue of vast historical and social dimensions will have been reduced to a simple matter of individual leaders seeking personal advantage and "taking advantage." And that is surely not the whole story of official Marxism-Leninism in *any* domain.

Our principal concern at this point is the present and possible future of human relationships as focal points of value in these countries, countries that are proving increasingly fascinating to philosophers and others interested in gender issues because of their generally more conservative ways, by comparison with "the West," in these very respects. (For instance, Eastern European attitudes toward homosexuality are probably on average even more intolerant than attitudes in Western countries, a certain machismo being regarded as the nearly unquestioned male norm.) One way of approaching this concern of ours is to ask with Freud, though in a more egalitarian manner and without his intended sarcasm, What do women *and* men want (in terms of human relationships)? But we cannot, as we shall see, leave it at the point of exploring merely what they want right now, at this moment in time.

The first thing to be said, I think, to those who ask this question is that women as a whole, like men as a whole, have diverse and often conflicting wishes. There is said to be a sizable number of women in the countries of Eastern and Central Europe, probably a larger proportion than in the West because of the differences in recent past history, who find the ideal of marrying a man of wealth and not working outside the home far more attractive than any alternative. Some of these same women, and no doubt some also among those who do harbor career aspirations, reject the idea of gender equality, either because they consider it inappropriate and impractical, maybe even "against nature," or because they feel that within the framework of the chivalric ideal of "woman on a pedestal" they will enjoy great advantages, or for both reasons combined. On the other hand, conferences on feminist issues and organizations of women insisting on more equal treatment proliferate. Men who wish to be responsive to "what women want" may at times express bewilderment at these conflicting tendencies and felt needs. Yet diversity is a fact of life, as is the ambivalence that permeates all serious human relationships.

If positive human relationships are, as I believe, a remaining potential locus of value when all the other former values of a society have failed (as I have heard the current situation described repeatedly particularly in Bulgaria), then this diversity is precisely what needs to be protected and strengthened. But this is just what conservative preachers of "a return to family values," of whom Eastern Europe has its share, cannot accept. Neither, on the other hand, can certain types of feminists, who simply condemn out of hand women who engage in various old-fashioned behaviors that they identify as typically "female."[22] The tolerance for diversity that I am advocating as the social norm requires a very high level of maturity in a society, far higher than the average of any society of which I am aware today. Yet the very combination of a relatively high level of education and the loss of confidence in most other values that characterizes today's East European populations suggests that social conditions *could* be favorable for promoting such tolerance. *Could* be, I repeat; I am speaking here of hypothetical possibilities, not existing realities.

One of the most immediate needs in this area of human relationships, as I perceive it, is to find ways to eliminate widespread practices of "sexual harassment" in those societies. This could be accomplished through education and discussion, together with strong legal action against the more egregious cases. At present, a large stock of anecdotal evidence has led me to conclude, practices falling under the rubric of sexual harassment, at least in its less extreme forms, are taken for granted by large segments of the populations. Stories abound about male superiors' tying important career decisions for female subordinates to their willingness to give sexual favors. But who am I, as an American, to preach about this? A long and all-too-well-known series of charges, countercharges, and betrayals over such matters in the recent history of the United States leaves most East Europeans, who have also read the newspaper stories, with the correct impression that American society has not yet found a reasonably satisfactory resolution to generations-old problems of injustices in the area of gender relations, either.[23] That new, unconventional models of behavior in this area, to be accepted or not according to the wishes of individual partners and groups, are needed in the wake of recent changes both in women's status and in reproductive technology seems obvious to me, and such new models would be particularly valuable to societies such as those of Eastern Europe in which interpersonal relationships are matters of enormous concern. But it seems equally obvious that there is as yet little agreement about this.

How realistic in any case, at present, are proposals to promote and ameliorate the values of human relationships? Of course there are still, in the countries of Central and Eastern Europe, plenty of smaller communities of persons with shared interests—artists, for example—within which positive human relationships (together with the inevitable jealousies, rifts, etc.) do flourish. Warm friendships among individuals with no blood ties remain commonplace. Even among strangers who find themselves together in, for example, vehicles of public transport the atmosphere is generally far from being one of overt hostility. And numerous couples, married and unmarried alike, are in fact quite aware of the importance of equality in such areas as sharing domestic tasks and act to at least *some* degree in accordance with this awareness. In opposition to all of this, however, are the realities of penury and economic stress, reinforced by the vastly increased sense of competition and the loss of material security that accompany the new official worldview of neoliberal capitalism. The result has been increased isolation, alienation, and mutual hostility among vast numbers of ordinary people. To repeat just one very mundane but significant example of how this works, entertainment of friends and dining out have, as I mentioned in chapter 5, become rare occasions for all but the most well-off strata of many of these societies. (The well-off strata, though small in percentage, it should be added, are still numerous enough, in absolute terms, to permit active restaurant industries to flourish in the larger cities.) Meanwhile, incidents of gross discrimination and of beatings and even killings of Gypsies and foreigners by so-called Skinheads and others in such diverse places as former East Germany, former Czechoslovakia,[24] and Serbia proliferate. Under such conditions, talk of genuine diversity and of ameliorating human relationships and elevating them to a central place among human values seems irredeemably utopian.

But then *any* talk of an alternative worldview, an alternative set of values, seems to take on a utopian aura at the present time. In my concluding chapter, I consider the war of worldviews.

Notes

1. "His whole philosophy he condensed into a phrase which he had recently coined during [a political meeting]—*The Altar, the Throne and the Cottage*." Cecil Driver, *Tory Radical: The Life of Richard Oastler* (New York: Oxford University Press, 1946), 203.

2. The film was shown, for one of the first times, at the international symposium, "Russia: Strategy of Development in the 3rd Millennium," Dubna, October 20, 1997, at which Academician Moiseyev was also honored with a special award from the Vernadsky Foundation. Simultaneous translation into English was provided.

3. Among the more accurate books, in my opinion, are two with the same principal title: Misha Glenny, *The Fall of Yugoslavia: The Third Balkan War* (London: Penguin Books, 1992); and Svetozar Stojanović, *The Fall of Yugoslavia: Why Communism Failed* (Amherst, N.Y.: Prometheus, 1997).

4. Benedict Anderson, *Imagined Communities: Reflections on the Origins and Spread of Nationalism* (London: Verso, 1995). The fact that this work, dealing mostly with East Asia and already somewhat out of date from a historical perspective, is so frequently cited in philosophical treatments of nationalism testifies to the comparative paucity of such treatments, which is surprising, given the prominence of the topic itself. One (of several) useful recent exception to this generalization is the special issue, "Philosophical Perspectives on National Identity," of *The Philosophical Forum* 28, nos. 1–2 (fall-winter 1996–97). The issue is edited by Omar Dahbour.

5. I am here thinking especially of Jürgen Habermas, *Faktizität und Geltung: Beiträge zur Diskurstheorie des Rechts und des demokratischen Rechtsstaats* (Frankfurt am Main: Suhrkamp, 1992) and *The New Conservatism: Cultural Criticism and the Historians' Debate*, ed. and trans. S. W. Nicholsen (Cambridge, Mass.: MIT Press, 1989).

6. Natalija Mićunović, "A Critique of Nationalism" (Ph.D. diss., Purdue University, 1996).

7. Martin J. Matuštík, *Postnational Identity: Critical Theory and Existential Philosophy in Habermas, Kierkegaard, and Havel* (New York: Guilford, 1993).

8. William L. McBride, "Clarifying 'Civil Society' and Creating Space for Civil Societies: From the Struggle against Nation-State Despotisms to the Critique of Despotic Transnationalisms," in *Resurrecting the Phoenix: Proceedings from the International Congress on Civil Society in South East Europe: Philosophical and Ethical Perspectives*, ed. David C. Durst, Maria Dimitrova, Alexander Gungov, and Borislava Vassileva (Sofia: EOS, 1998).

9. See Julia Kristeva, *Nations without Nationalism* (New York: Columbia University Press, 1993); Jason Hill, "Creating the Self: Toward a Cosmopolitan Identity" (Ph.D. diss., Purdue University, 1998).

10. I argue in favor of taking a major step in this direction by effectively eliminating emigration and immigration restrictions worldwide (while enforcing existing workers' rights to work, as stipulated in *The Universal Declaration of Human Rights*), in "The Rights of 'Aliens' and of Other Others," in *Chal-*

lenges to Law at the End of the 20th Century: Rights, ed. Rex Martin and Gerhard Sprenger; *Proceedings of the International Association for Philosophy of Law and Social Philosophy (IVR) 1, ARSP-Beiheft 67*, Martin and Sprenger, eds. (Stuttgart: Franz Steiner Verlag, 1997): 192–99.

11. Rorty uses, with approval, the expression "postmodern bourgeois democracy" and applauds the idea of "philosophy *in the service of* democratic politics—as a contribution to the attempt to achieve what Rawls calls 'reflective equilibrium' between our instinctive reactions to contemporary problems and the general principles on which we have been reared." Richard Rorty, *Contingency, Irony, and Solidarity* (Cambridge, Eng.: Cambridge University Press, 1989), 196. Elsewhere he says that "we heirs of the Enlightenment think of enemies of liberal democracy like Nietzsche or Loyola as, to use Rawls's word, 'mad.'" "The Priority of Democracy to Philosophy," in *The Virginia Statute for Religious Freedom*, ed. Merrill D. Peterson and Robert C. Vaughan (Cambridge, Eng.: Cambridge University Press, 1988), 266. These two citations are, it seems to me, illustrative of a general attitude, one that has become even more manifest in his latest work.

12. The following passage is typical: "We are to be missionaries of civilization, [they say,] and to bear the white man's burden, painful as it often is. We must sow our ideals, plant our order, impose our God. The individual lives are nothing. Our duty and our destiny call, and civilization must go on.

"Could there be a more damning indictment of that whole bloated idol termed 'modern civilization' than this amounts to?" William James, "The Philippine Tangle," in *A William James Reader*, ed. Gay Wilson Allen (1899; Boston: Houghton Mifflin, 1971), 225.

13. Are these two enterprises, explaining and justifying, in some sense the same? In other words, is it perhaps true, in some ultimate sense, that *tout comprendre, c'est tout pardonner*? This question arose during a public discussion of an East European intellectual whose evolving political commitments, widely scorned and criticized by members of the audience who had known him or at least known about him, I had been attempting to analyze and explain. I pointed out that things similar to what at least one questioner said concerning my approach, to wit, that it was exculpating, had been said of Sartre's treatment of Stalin in the unfinished second volume of his *Critique of Dialectical Reason*, despite Sartre's obviously quite negative judgment of Stalin and his regime. Some members of the audience strongly defended my approach, maintaining that too much sheer, unthinking condemnation without analysis is all too common under current circumstances. That, of course, is also my view. But it is, I think, true in the final analysis that a sort of continuum obtains between explanation and justification. Although judgments that are almost purely condemnatory remain possible, a careful exploration of the actor's reasons for reprehensible conduct will almost inevitably render such judgments less absolutist in nature.

14. A concrete example of such sentiments in operation today, a particularly troubling one at that, is to be found in the refusal of some regimes, particularly in Asia (China, India, Pakistan), to sign a proposed "nuclear nonproliferation

treaty" as long as it permits those countries now known to be in possession of nuclear weapons, most notably the United States and Russia of course, to remain in possession of them. Nearly everyone, I would like to say "every rational person," now thinks of a world entirely free of nuclear weapons as a future ideal. But there are many who understandably regard a world in which only a few powerful countries have such weapons, with the most powerful having by far the most, as very far from ideal. And so two bitter national rivals, India and Pakistan, made the decision to initiate nuclear weapons tests in May 1998.

15. The expression "one world" was used (in English) by Sartre in a significant way in his *Critique of Dialectical Reason*. (It was also, among its many other earlier uses, the title of a book by Wendell Willkie, the Republican candidate who lost the 1940 U.S. Presidential elections.) The exploration of its implications serves as the theme of the final chapter of my book *Social and Political Philosophy* (New York: Paragon, 1994), 136–48.

16. In the case of Bosnia, however, it must be said that Alija Izetbegović had been an open advocate of some such Muslim religious revival long before he assumed the presidency of this newly independent state.

17. Karl Marx, "Contribution to the Critique of Hegel's *Philosophy of Right:* Introduction," in *The Marx-Engels Reader*, ed. Robert C. Tucker, 2d ed. (New York: Norton, 1978), 54.

18. This attitude is in keeping with Marx's insistence, in his *Critique of the Gotha Program*, and with Lenin's gloss on the latter in his *State and Revolution*, that the first postrevolutionary phase of communist society would necessarily involve people who had been strongly socialized and habituated in a traditional "bourgeois" manner and that they would have to be taken and dealt with as they were. Religious practices, however, are not discussed at any length in either work.

19. Hegel's very frequent characterization of religion as "picture thinking," which nevertheless constitutes one of the highest developments of spirit, runs along similar lines.

20. Marx, *Economic and Philosophic Manuscripts of 1844*, in *Marx-Engels Reader*, 83–84.

21. These issues and perceptions are extensively discussed in *Gender Politics and Post-Communism: Reflections from Eastern Europe and the Former Soviet Union*, ed. Nanette Funk and Magda Muller (New York: Routledge, 1993).

22. These issues are treated with great sensitivity in Sandra Bartky, *Femininity and Domination: Studies in the Phenomenology of Oppression* (New York: Routledge), 1990.

23. In much of Western, as well as Eastern, Europe there is a tendency, even among otherwise progressive men and some women, to make fun of the "political correctness" of Americans in the area of rules governing sexual comportment. This is due in some measure to ignorance of the facts, together with the heavy propaganda of a generally conservative press that makes use of isolated stories from the United States about truly inappropriate and ridiculous interpretations of what prohibiting sexual harassment entails. In Eastern Europe it has

sometimes fallen to me to explain at some length, to intelligent people, just what the expression "sexual harassment" means. But none of this amounts to an endorsement, by women or even men of good faith, of most of the behavior that falls under this concept.

24. Concerning the Gypsies, see, for example, Aviezer Tucker, "The New Jews," *Telos* 98–99 (winter 1993-fall 1994): 209–15.

Chapter Seven

Worldviews: From One Materialism to Another?

I continue to endorse the minimal underlying premise of chapter 4 to the effect that philosophy and political practice should and do have something to do with one another. I would therefore have liked to be able to conclude, after having raised one final time the question of alternative worldviews—nothing less than the question of the meaning of human life itself as we look towards its future in the Third Millennium—by offering a proposed realistic general strategy for moving from the tawdry present of profit-driven "globalization" to something better.

The sticking point is the word "realistic." I, like many before me, could attempt to construct a utopia, and in fact I think that the construction of utopias can be a very valuable type of philosophical exercise.[1] But to do so here would be out of keeping with the place and time upon which this book has focused. David Schweickart, for instance, offers some hope for a future transition to a market socialist economic system (or rather, systems, since he very controversially and I think anachronistically assumes an indefinite continuation of nation-states and even finds this beneficial in some respects) which he now labels "economic democracy." He gives reasoned (if admittedly not always overwhelmingly conclusive) arguments, over many carefully constructed pages, in favor of the system that he endorses vis-à-vis others, but the few pages that he devotes to the feasibility of its being adopted strike me as among the weakest and most halfhearted in the book.[2] How could it be otherwise? The historically unprecedented power of the forces reinforcing the present world order, their fierce, even zealous, sense of self-interest that dismisses critics out of hand, and their ever increasing control of all the media combine to make it virtually unthinkable that there will be a serious change in direction in the near future, barring a widespread apocalyptic conversion of mentalities,[3] that is, a worldwide "inner revolution," or an *extremely* severe worldwide cataclysm. The first of these possibilities strikes me as being as close to unthinkable as any historical scenario could ever be, and the second, alas much more thinkable,[4] would entail so much additional human suffering as to render it humanly undesirable regardless of the splendor of the brave new world that *might* await humanity on the other side.

The depth of my pessimism about offering practical suggestions for a better future resembles the pessimism of Herbert Marcuse at the end of *One-Dimensional Man*. But it is being expressed almost a quarter-century later in the wake of global changes that make the Western society with which he was primarily concerned appear touchingly innocent in many respects by comparison with ours.[5] My pessimism can be attributed in part to the venue in which I am completing the draft of this book: Sofia, Bulgaria, at the end of a three-month residence. The "crisis" in Bulgaria, as everyone calls it, which is undoubtedly considerably more severe than in most of the former Soviet Bloc countries of Eastern and Central Europe or even, in certain respects, former Yugoslavia, but probably comparable to that in Russia itself and some of the former Soviet republics, shows few signs of abating. No one, not even a director of the International Monetary Fund, can with a straight face call an 80–90 percent poverty level optimal. And no one expects a sudden or dramatic amelioration, if any at all. If, for example, all the CEOs in the United States were to donate all of their annual salaries, beyond what they really need to maintain a quite lavish lifestyle, to the national treasury of this small country and a fair distribution plan were to be worked out and implemented, then Bulgaria would be awash with money. But then if pigs could fly bacon would be at a premium.

Thus I have given advance warning against expecting a "happy ending." But that does not mean that we are done with fairy tales. Dialectical materialism was one such fairy tale, a "grand narrative" as the postmodernist thinkers put it. We seldom hear it recounted any longer, but tall stories about the magic of the market have come to serve as worthy substitutes. Dialectical materialism in its so-called orthodox form, the form that sustained employment for thousands of philosophers and so-called philosophers in this part of the world over several decades (since courses in it were mandatory), held that nature itself functioned according to relatively predictable basic dialectical patterns (the transformation of quantity into quality and vice versa, the interpenetration of opposites, and the negation of the negation—so went the basic mantra[6]) and that human beings, as special cases in the evolutionary development of universal matter, followed the same patterns in complex but comprehensible ways. There were many ingenious stratagems for explaining apparent historical deviations from these patterns.

Despite all the misrepresentations and illusions that were involved in this "orthodox" approach, I continue to believe that in the pursuit of some of those stratagems important new understandings of the sociohistorical world were generated. In a certain sense the philosophy of Marx, even when transformed from a critical analysis of the dynamic, emerging world system of his time into the fairy tale "diamat" (a bit like Rapunzel), to which a kind of universal truth was attributed, was and remains in advance of much of the *corpus* of philosophical thinking in this area. But it was the broad ontological dogma that this alleged wisdom of the ages was a *materialism*, meaning (it was supposed) something opposite to *idealism* and entailing a disbelief in the existence of *spiritual* entities, which, far more than disagreements about particular historical explanations, underlay and was used to justify much of the persecution of those, especially intellectuals, who had what was thought to be a different worldview. ("Idealist" became the epithet of choice to express severe intellectual condemnation.) The most bitter irony in this stems from the fact that, as a more careful and reflective analysis soon reveals, all three of the italicized concepts, particularly the first, materialism, are at best ambiguous and at worst relatively empty of content—allegedly clear-cut *prises de position* that virtually vanish under scrutiny. Hence much of the literature of the times and places in which diamat reigned supreme, including even writings of severe critics who were nevertheless constrained to take it seriously, now reads as something childishly formulaic (no offense to children intended), catechetical, an easy fill-in-the-blanks questionnaire based on certain vague and dubious axioms that were taken as being beyond dispute.

Unfortunately, much of contemporary professional Western philosophy, in ontology, philosophy of mind, ethics, social and political philosophy, and indeed virtually all areas, exhibits a comparable conformism, obsession with certain concepts and formulas, and acceptance of certain axioms as beyond dispute. Philosophy of religion courses that begin with the announcement that the existence of God will not be brought into question, business ethics courses that take for granted the morality of the capitalist system, and political philosophy courses that treat the nation-state as a given may be regarded as paradigmatic. That many Western philosophers behave in this way, thereby betraying what I have always regarded, along with Marx, as philosophy's basic mission to engage in "a *ruthless criticism of everything existing*,"[7] is by no means incompatible with their maintaining high, sometimes even dazzling, levels of technical proficiency. Such proficiency was not unheard of among at least a few professors of diamat, either.

The phrase "from one materialism to another" is a natural one for observers of the transformations in Eastern Europe to use. It is based, of course, on a play of words, since dialectical materialism did make ontological claims, however difficult to pin down precisely,[8] whereas the "New Materialism" refers, once again, to a certain set of *values*, which are *also* difficult to pin down but are in any case expected to lead, fairy tale-like, to a happy ending. For most people today in Bulgaria and many elsewhere, it is a materialism of *lack* and of the envy of this lack, rather than one of possession. In the last analysis, perhaps, a good case can be made to the effect that, contrary to appearances, "materialism" in this widely accepted Western form ultimately *embodies* or *incarnates* lack, the "void as object of will" of which Nietzsche spoke. Let us consider this point further.

What the new (to Eastern Europe, at least) materialism means is the implementation, in daily practice and to the extent possible within one's means, of egoism, that is, the commitment to maximizing one's immediate personal gratification with the aid of as many expensive "toys" as possible—a commitment that is assumed to require accumulating as much wealth as one can. The fact that generalizing this principle will necessarily lead to conflict and contradiction in a society of more than one person is a point that writers in ethics have made untold numbers of times but that still seems to be discounted. Neither does it seem to matter that the (human) subject itself, the supposed *agent* of all this self-gratification, has been deconstructed by the postmodern movement, so that its very existence and nature have become more problematic than ever. In Bulgaria a popular magazine is called *Egoizm*, while polls indicate the tremendous popularity, among some young people, of a criminal ("mafioso") who has been particularly successful in realizing these materialist "values." Where, as the traditionalists also ask, will it all end? The answer to this question is simple: nowhere. As Plato and Aristotle already saw quite well, πλεονεξια, the quest for maximum ego gratification, can have no end. It involves a bad kind of infinity that has the void as its object.

If we set aside old prejudices about values and agree, as I have been urging throughout my discussions of values, that they are human creations rather than natural givens, what is so "bad" about this materialism/egoism? If we assume that the material girls and material boys who are committed to it can find pragmatic compromises, on an ad hoc basis and without denying the fundamental contradictoriness of the view on a philosophical level, that allow them to fend off mutual destruction, then what's the problem? Perhaps the best reply (a very Aristotelean one, as it happens) to this question is that such a worldview entails refusing to explore many interesting and intriguing possibilities that would otherwise be open to human beings as human. It certainly entails, among other things, forgetting philosophy, since philosophy simply cannot be considered a materialistic pursuit in the value-laden sense of the word materialism, even for those philosophers who may consider themselves "materialists" in an ontological sense. Taken strictly, the new materialist worldview also entails eliminating or at least minimizing research activities, in whatever discipline, that cost money but cannot be shown to have direct applicability to the task of increasing gratification except for the tiny minority of dedicated researchers themselves. This is the policy path that has in fact been followed, in large measure, in many of the countries of Eastern Europe, particularly Russia itself, in the wake of economic collapse and restructuring—reducing moneys available for scientific research and education to a bare-bones level, disregarding almost entirely the need to keep pace intellectually through library acquisitions, and compensating the remaining researchers and educators at a poverty level.[9] In short, in the universe of the new materialism, a word such as "intellectual" (the noun), which in former times had a very high status in principle even though this status was often negated in actual practice, appears strange at best and at worst laughable or ridiculous.

These anti-intellectual developments are taking place, contradictorily enough, in a decade in which computer technology is obviously revolutionizing life throughout much of the world in a direction that permits a previously inconceivable expansion of knowledge and communication. Surely one of the (many) reasons for the almost unprecedented collapse of a whole system and way of life that has been the inspiration for the present book was the refusal of Communist leaderships to wholeheartedly encourage this technology in its early phases, even though strong foundations for it existed in Eastern Europe (especially, as a matter of fact, in Bulgaria).[10] Their reasons were obvious, in a sense: The extremely free communication that we now see occurring via the Internet was a very unwelcome prospect to people for whom secrecy and control were highest priorities. But their policy of suppression of dissent thereby also caused a suppression of potential technological development in the very area in which such development was taking place elsewhere in a very fast and radical way. Although computer literacy is fairly widespread in Eastern Europe today, the area lags well behind Western countries in the accessibility of these tools, which have become such crucial prerequisites for research and general intellectual exploration beyond the sphere of material gratification.

Cyberspace technology and the new ways of thinking that accompany it are concrete (if that word is at all appropriate in this context!) embodiments of an idea—the noosphere—that began to be developed by two interestingly disparate scientist/philosophers who were briefly acquainted in Paris in the 1920s, Jesuit anthropologist Teilhard de Chardin and Russian physicist V. I. Vernadsky. The noosphere is to be conceived as a new era in cosmic history (of which human history is only a part, albeit a pivotal one), in which mind and the mental are becoming increasingly prominent relative to the biological and lower spheres.[11] For Teilhard, cosmic evolution had a mystic, theological outcome in what he called "Point Omega," while Vernadsky's thinking, which coexisted uneasily with Marxist-Leninist orthodoxy during the Soviet era, has now become a rallying point for some who (not entirely without reason) regard Russia as having a very special historical role; but we need not necessarily accept either of these kinds of interpretation in order to share with them and with a number of other twentieth-century thinkers of broad vision the sense that a truly radical change is taking place. New dimensions of mental reality are rapidly being discovered, which transcend by many orders of magnitude the familiar domain of ordinary sense experience but cannot be understood in terms of any of mainstream Western philosophy's traditional ontological conceptions of mind—Greek νους, Kantian reason, Enlightenment rationality, Cartesian soul, Hegelian spirit, and so on. All of the latter are being rendered outmoded, and new questions about the meaning of life itself are being posed. These profound changes are occurring simultaneously with the burgeoning of the new materialism, the triumphant advance of Coca-Cola culture, and the stunning acceleration of the processes of economic "globalization." Indeed, the computer technology associated with the discovery of these new dimensions of mental reality, as I have expressed it, has greatly facilitated the "progress" of the cultural, or counter-cultural, and economic developments that I have been describing.

We therefore need to acknowledge, it seems to me, that a confluence of historical trends, the future direction of which I neither pretend to be able to predict nor believe any contemporary of mine capable of predicting with confidence, has created living contradictions within our present world that dwarf the historical contradictions discerned by Hegel, Marx, and others in the dialectical tradition of the philosophy of history. These contradictory trends are manifested with special clarity in parts of Eastern Europe as the twentieth century of the Christian era draws to a close. Abjection prevails, injustices abound and multiply, and all the while wealth and brute power of unprecedented dimensions are accumulating in select sites and milieux. Edifying schemes of global redistribution may be proposed as ways of overcoming the most extreme of these contradictions, but they remain merely edifying and impotent.

I am unimpressed by the approaching Millennium. Whatever significance it has stems from the combined historical contingencies that one religion among many has managed to make its calendar the calendar of record and that one of many possible numbering systems, the decimal system, has come to be universally adopted. I regard talk of an end of history, which sometimes accompanies millennial talk, as meaningless except in one relatively banal sense: the conceivable nuclear or other catastrophe that might extinguish all human life.[12] Apart from this quintessentially unattractive possibility, then, there is no temporal escape from the highly (but still merely mundanely) unattractive realities of the present. Some of the countries with which I have been concerned here may well become appendages of the European Community and of NATO—avid if still somewhat peripheral participants in the hegemonic consumerist "Coca-Cola culture" to which I have been alluding. In others, such as Bulgaria and Russia and other former Soviet republics, there will *at best* be some slow, gradual amelioration of real material conditions. But their short-term prognoses are *not* very good, even in the judgment of some former would-be economist-kings who then became, at least for a time, economist-cheerleaders. Ominously, the cheerleading has begun to subside.

Despair, on the other hand, is incoherent in the face of a decision to continue living and therefore, by definition, forming projects that look to the future. Despite the systematic downgrading of finance allocation for education, research, and the arts that has characterized most of the past decade and has contributed so much to demoralization among the intellectual leaderships in Eastern Europe and virtually worldwide, some individuals, young people among them, continue stubbornly to resist these discouragements and to pursue creative activities and engage in serious critical thinking—"philosophical reflection" in precisely the sense intended by this book's title—about their/our obviously skewed world. So, although I refuse to indulge in idle chatter about "hope,"[13] I trust that it will not seem offensive to the many who are suffering if I conclude by reaffirming that the resources of the human spirit (art, philosophy in the broadest sense, the sciences, and in short all that is to be understood as culture), enhanced as they are now being by the developing new dimensions of mind to which I have referred, are still available for those who retain the strength and courage to *transcend* the new materialism that has supplanted the old within the venerable societies to which this book has been dedicated.

Notes

1. A good case for this has been made by Erin McKenna, "A Process Model of Utopia: Revising Models of Utopia in Light of Pragmatist and Feminist Perspectives" (Ph.D. diss., Purdue University, 1992).

2. David Schweickart, *Against Capitalism* Boulder: Westview, 1996), 282–92.

3. Sartre's reflections on the possibility of "radical conversion," discussed in chapter 3, reach a kind of *reductio* point in his posthumously published *Notebooks for an Ethics* (Cahiers pour une Morale), in which he recognizes that a simultaneous radical conversion of everyone, which would be the "end of history" and the coming into existence of an ethical world, is an infinitely remote possibility. See *Notebooks for an Ethics*, trans. D. Pellauer (Chicago: University of Chicago Press, 1992), 88.

4. Such a cataclysm could take the form of an exchange of nuclear weapons or a biological or chemical catastrophe of global dimensions but falling short of total annihilation of the human race, or perhaps even a major economic crash on a world scale comparable to the disruption brought about within Albania by the collapse of a nationwide pyramid investment scheme.

5. Marcuse concludes this generally pessimistic work, published on the eve of his late-life rise to prominence during the period of worldwide protest against the conformist tendencies that he identified, with a citation from Walter Benjamin to the effect that "it is only for the sake of those without hope that hope is given to us." *One-Dimensional Man* (Boston: Beacon, 1964), 257. There is no reference in the text to the fact that Benjamin took his life not too long after writing this.

6. The canonical source of this was Friedrich Engels, *Dialectics of Nature* (New York: International Publishers, 1940), 26.

7. This expression is taken, as noted in chapter 4, from Karl Marx's important letter of September 1843 to his friend Arnold Ruge. See *The Marx-Engels Reader*, ed. Robert C. Tucker, 2d ed. (New York: Norton, 1978), 13.

8. In saying this, I by no means intend to imply an oblique condemnation of all ontology, simply of *bad* ontology. In fact, as I have frequently argued elsewhere, I believe, contrary to what Rawls and a number of other contemporary writers claim, that it is impossible in the last analysis to completely disassociate one's social and political philosophy from ontological commitments—notions about what is ultimately real—even if those notions are relegated to the status of unarticulated assumptions.

9. Academician N. N. Moiseyev, mentioned at the beginning of the previous chapter, is no doubt typical of many Russian intellectuals in regarding this mutilation of research and education budgets as the most unforgivable of the legacies of the Gorbachev era.

10. Some of the most interesting analyses of the relationship between computer technology and both Marxism and Communist regimes are those of J. C. Nyíri, to whom I referred in my introductory chapter. For an early study of this relationship, see his article "Some Marxian Themes in the Age of Information"

in *Perspectives on Ideas and Reality*, ed. J. C. Nyíri (Budapest: Filozófiai Posztgraduális és Információs Központ, 1990), 55–65.

11. It was apparently a third scientist acquainted with both Teilhard and Vernadsky, Edouard LeRoy, who actually coined the terms "noosphere" and "biosphere."

12. Sartre makes some brief but telling remarks about the possible catastrophe that might abruptly bring about the end "of the story" of human history, the result of which, in the absence of any person or being *"to close the eyes of humanity,"* would be that no one would (will) ever know "the truth" of history, in his posthumously published *Vérité et existence* (Paris: Gallimard, 1989), 132.

13. See my review of *Hope Now*, by Jean-Paul Sartre and Benny Lévy, in *Radical Philosophy Review of Books* 14 (1996): 13–19.

Index

abjection, 92–94, 97, 106, 130
abortion, 41, 87–88, 114
addiction, 108
Albania, 83, 113, 132n4
alienation, 56–57, 120
Allende, Salvador, 32
Althusser, Louis, 27
Arendt, Hannah, 23n15
Aristotle, 1–2, 6, 14, 58, 128

bad faith, 48–52
base/superstructure model, 26, 82
belief. *See* faith
Bloch, Ernst, 61n8
Bolsheviks, 78n10, 93, 105
Bosnia, 57, 96, 112
Brandt, Willy, 57
Bulgaria, 5–7, 19, 33, 89, 98, 112, 114–16, 119, 126, 128, 131

capitalism, 27–28, 30–32, 34, 37, 60, 73, 75–76, 83–86, 95, 120
Central European University, 76
Chile, 32
civil society, 35–38, 97–98
clergy, 114
Coca-Cola culture. *See* culture
coercion, 69, 75, 84
commercialization, 83
Communism, 16, 33–34, 48–49
Communist Manifesto, 14–15
Communist Party, 2, 6, 8, 14, 16, 20, 34–35, 47, 51, 59

community, 57, 82, 96, 108, 120
Constellations, 23n14
contraception, 50–51, 87
Ćosić, Dobrica, 78n6
cosmopolitanism, 109, 111
crime, 28–29
critique, 71, 127
Croatia, 25, 34, 83, 112, 115
culture, 31, 36, 84, 92–94, 97–98, 109, 131; Coca-Cola culture, 78n11, 93, 130–31
cynicism, 20–21, 30, 41, 82, 94–95
Czechoslovakia, 5, 7, 18–19, 66, 87, 107, 120; Czech Republic, 74, 76, 89

Danas, 11n5, 25
decentering, 40
democracy, 5, 33–35, 39–40, 69, 73, 76, 85, 95–97, 105, 107; participatory, 40
Derrida, Jacques, 39
Descartes, René, 70–71
determinism, 28
dialectical materialism ("Diamat"), 10, 15, 47, 69, 126–27
dissidence, 48, 57, 66
Djilas, Milovan, 20

East Germany, 5, 8, 13, 39, 53, 88–89, 120
economic domain, 25–31; economists, 74–77, 84

efficiency-for-profit, 86–89
egoism, 128
Engels, Friedrich, 14, 16, 79n17
ethics, 82, 103n31, 127–28
Europe, Eastern and Central, meanings of, 11n1
explanation, 7–8, 106–07, 118

faith, 50–51, 54, 114–15
family, 116–17
fetishism of commodities, 31, 84, 86
filioque question, 115
Flaubert, Gustave, 55
forgiveness, 89, 122n13
freedom, 82–85
free market. *See* market
Friedman, Milton, 32, 99n6
Friedrich, Carl, 23n15
fundamental change, 6, 7, 42–43, 46n30, 47
fundamental project, 54–55

generational differences, 94
globalization, 91, 125, 130
Golubović, Zagorka, 62n21
Gorbachev, Mikhail, 66, 132n9
guilt, 89
Gypsies, 88, 120

Habermas, Jürgen, 103n28
Havel, Václav, 5, 33, 66, 74, 108
Hegel, G. W. F., 14, 20, 37, 59, 101n14, 102n26, 123n19
Heidegger, Martin, 62n24
history, 5, 13–14, 22n2, 131; historical inevitability, 21; historical memory, 89–90, 109; historical progress, 42
Hobbes, Thomas, 35, 58, 77
homosexuality, 49, 118
Hook, Sydney, 16
humanism, 56–57
Hungary, 4, 18, 21, 41, 111

idealism, 2, 68–69, 127
ideals, 4, 43n4, 53, 95
ideological domain, 38–43, 59

intellectuals, 47–48, 65–66, 70, 129
international banking organizations, 97; International Monetary Fund, 74–75, 126
Internet, 129
Inter-University Centre, 4, 6, 19
Izetbegović, Alija, 123n16

James, William, 110
John Paul II, Pope, 45n24, 50–51, 86–87
justice, 30, 91–95, 120, 130

Kadar, Janoš, 4
Kant, Immanuel, 58, 69, 71
Karadžić, Radovan, 96
Kharin, Yuri A., 15
Khrushchev, Nikita, 18
Kierkegaard, Søren, 60n4, 108
Kołakowski, Leszek, 55–57, 66
Korčula, School of, 19–20
Korsch, Karl, 15–16
Kosovo, 106

legitimacy, 30
Lenin, V. I., 14, 61n9, 68–70, 123n18
liberation theology, 87
Locke, John, 37
Lombardo-Radice, Luigi, 44n7
Lukács, Georg, 13, 15–16
lustration, 89
Lyotard, Jean-François, 46n28

MacIntyre, Alasdair, 81, 98
mafia, 29
majority rule, 26
Marcuse, Herbert, 126
market, 5, 32–33, 39–40, 75, 84, 126
market socialism, 125
Marković, Mihailo, 17, 23n14, 57–58, 66
Marx, Karl, 30, 37–38, 40, 68, 71–73, 77, 113, 115, 123n18, 127; early writings of, 16, 117
Marxism, 1, 4, 6, 26, 38–39, 56; Marxism-Leninism, 1, 4, 13–22, 28, 31–32, 40, 47, 50, 52–53, 55,

61n9, 70, 73, 82, 115, 117–18, 127; Marxist-Christian dialogue, 87; post-Marxism, 109
Matuštík, Martin Beck, 108
Mešić, Stipe, 6
Mićunović, Dragoljub, 62n21, 66
Mićunović, Natalija, 108
Milošević, Slobodan, 57
Moiseyev, N. N., 105, 132n9
Moore, G. E., 60

nationalism, 17, 41–42, 57, 106–11
NATO (North Atlantic Treaty Organization), 94, 111, 131
Newman, John Henry Cardinal, 54
"New Class." *See nomenklatura*
Nietzsche, Friedrich, 89, 98, 128
nomenklatura, 9, 20, 29, 88, 90–91
noosphere, 129–30
Nozick, Robert, 33, 92
Nyíri, J. C., 4, 21

Oastler, Richard, 105, 116
ontology, 127–28
open society, 68, 73, 75–76, 90
opportunism, 48, 53–54
Orthodox Christianity, 11n1, 112, 114

pensioners, 27, 117
Petrović, Gajo, 17, 34, 48
Pinochet, A., 32
Plato, 6, 36, 58, 65–68, 128
Poland, 3, 13, 18, 41, 43n1, 54–56, 74, 86–87, 111–12, 114–15
political domain, 31–38
political liberalism, 69
Popper, Karl, 68, 76
postmodernism, 13, 39–41, 46n28, 59, 109, 126, 128
pragmatism, 110
praxis (concept), 17
Praxis (journal), 17, 23n14
Praxis group, 3, 17–18, 34, 53, 74
Praxis International, 23n14
predictability, 8, 21, 28, 130
privacy, 60n1

privatization, 27–28, 32, 74–75, 90–91
Prohić, Eleonora, 11n5
property, 29
prostitution, 88
public goods, 84
publishing industry, 61n7

Qadaffi, Muammar, 45n24
Que faire?, 21, 97

racism, 93, 107
radical conversion, 49, 54
Rawls, John, 78n12, 91, 132n8
Raynova, Yvanka, 6, 13
Reagan, Ronald, 32
reflection theory of cognition, 69
religion, 41, 54–55, 111–16
repression, 14, 34, 88
ressentiment. *See* revenge
revenge, 88–91
Rocoeur, Paul, 100n12
Roman Catholicism, 11n1, 41, 50–52, 86–88, 114–15
Romania, 88
Rorty, Richard, 46n28, 63n30, 78n12, 110
Rousseau, Jean-Jacques, 45n26, 103n27
Russia, 29, 33, 47, 74, 83, 91, 105, 112, 116, 126, 129–31

Sachs, Jeffrey, 74
Sarajevo, 4, 102n25
Sartre, Jean-Paul, 4, 11n5, 24n15, 45n24, 48–50, 54–55, 103n31, 122n13, 132n3
Schengen accord, 93, 102n21
Schweickart, David, 125
self-management, 17
Serbia, 42, 57–58, 102n26, 108, 112, 115, 120
sexuality, 87–88, 108; sexual harassment, 119–20
skepticism, 35, 59
slavery, 30

socialism, 5, 9, 29–30, 34, 56–57; "really existing socialism," 43n4, 53
Socrates, 65, 67–68
Sofia, 5
Solidarity. *See Solidarnosc*
Solidarnosc, 3, 36, 55, 66
Soros, George, 76–77, 97
sovereignty, 75
Sovietology, 22
Soviet Union, 13, 15, 18, 36, 106
spirit, human, 116, 127, 131
St. Augustine, 54
St. Paul, 54–55
St. Petersburg, 93
Stalin, J., 15–18, 32, 61n9, 112–13, 122n13
Stein, Edith, 54
Stojanović, Svetozar, 66
superstructure. *See* base/superstructure model

Tamás, Gaspar Miklos̆, 66
Teilhard de Chardin, 130
Thatcher, Margaret, 74, 105
Third World, 93
totalitarianism, 9, 17–19, 23n15, 36, 47, 68, 73, 97, 118

transnational corporations, 98, 109–11
transvaluation of values, 82
Trotsky, L., 82
truth commissions, 90

Ukraine, 76
utopianism, 72–73, 120, 125

Varna, School of, 5, 20
Vernadsky, V. I., 130
virtues, 81, 98
visas, 93
Vrhnika (Slovenia), 2

Wałensa, Lech, 36, 66
war, 6, 68, 96
Western Marxism, 16, 53
Winter Palace, 93
Wolf, Markus, 88
women's issues, 87, 114, 117–20

Yeltsin, Boris, 34, 43n1
Young, Iris, 92
Yugoslavia, 2, 6, 17, 19, 21, 33, 41, 44, 90, 106, 111–12, 126

Želev, Želiu, 66

About the Author

William L. McBride is a professor of philosophy at Purdue University and the author and editor of books and articles about Jean-Paul Sartre, Marx and Marxism, social and political philosophy, the philosophy of law, phenomenology, and existentialism. He was cofounder of the North American Sartre Society and has served, at various times, as its director, as executive cosecretary of the Society for Phenomenology and Existential Philosophy (SPEP), as president of the Société Américaine de Philosophie de Langue Française, and as chair of the Committee for International Cooperation of the American Philosophical Association and member of its Board of Directors. His current positions include that of vice president of the North American Society for Social Philosophy and member of the Comité Directeur of the Fédération Internationale des Sociétés de Philosophie (FISP). He has been named Chevalier in the Ordre des Palmes Académiques by the French government and served as a Fulbright lecturer in Bulgaria in fall 1998.

www.ingramcontent.com/pod-product-compliance
Lightning Source LLC
Chambersburg PA
CBHW031553300426
44111CB00006BA/304